Charles A. Wimer

Complete Medical Record of President Garfield's Case

Charles A. Wimer

Complete Medical Record of President Garfield's Case

ISBN/EAN: 9783743324923

Manufactured in Europe, USA, Canada, Australia, Japa

Cover: Foto ©ninafisch / pixelio.de

Manufactured and distributed by brebook publishing software (www.brebook.com)

Charles A. Wimer

Complete Medical Record of President Garfield's Case

COMPLETE MEDICAL RECORD

OF

PRESIDENT GARFIELD'S CASE,

CONTAINING ALL OF THE

OFFICIAL BULLETINS,

From the Date of the Shooting to the Day of His Death,

TOGETHER WITH THE

OFFICIAL AUTOPSY,

MADE SEPTEMBER 20, 1881,

AND A DIAGRAM SHOWING THE COURSE TAKEN BY THE BALL.

Compiled from the Records of the Executive Mansion.

WASHINGTON, D. C.
CHAS. A. WIMER, PUBLISHER.
1881.

Entered according to act of Congress, in the year 1881, by
CHAS. A. WIMER,
In the Office of the Librarian of Congress at Washington.

PREFACE.

This volume is the result of a careful compilation of the official record kept in President Garfield's case, and is issued in the present form (without any additions, the nature of historical or other incidental information) in order that it may preserve in its entirety a complete compendium of the official utterances of the physicians in charge of the case; thus making it an authentic reference-book for the medical profession and general reader.

The grateful acknowledgments of the compiler are extended to Mr. J. Stanley Brown, Private Secretary to the late President Garfield, for the material aid he has so courteously afforded, and through whose coöperation the early publication of this volume is rendered possible.

THE COMPILER.

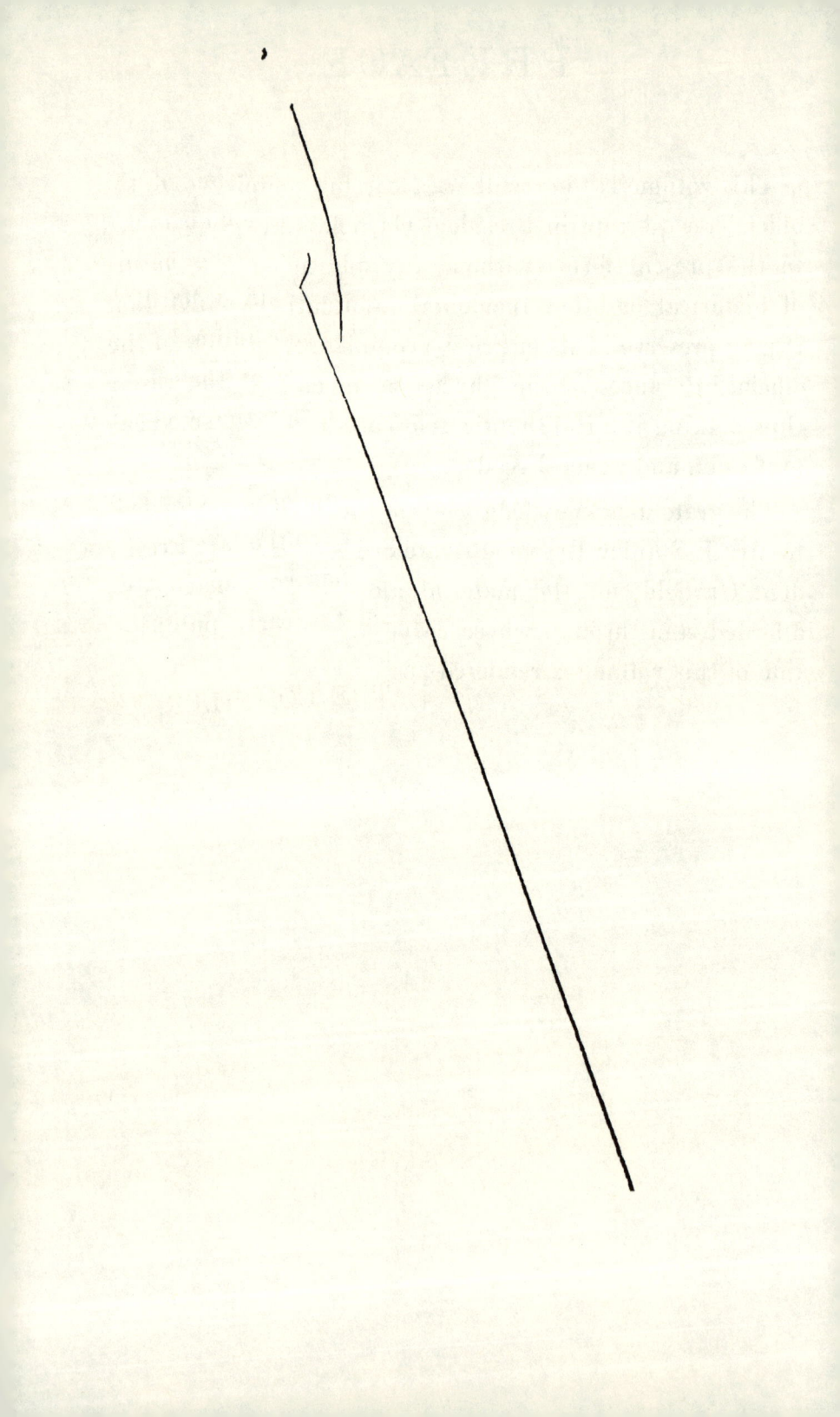

COMPLETE MEDICAL RECORD

OF

PRESIDENT GARFIELD'S CASE,

CONTAINING ALL OF THE

OFFICIAL BULLETINS,

From the Date of the Shooting to the Day of His Death,

TOGETHER WITH THE

OFFICIAL AUTOPSY,

MADE SEPTEMBER 20, 1881,

AND A DIAGRAM SHOWING THE COURSE TAKEN BY THE BALL.

Compiled from the Records of the Executive Mansion.

WASHINGTON, D. C.
CHAS. A. WIMER, PUBLISHER.
1881.

Entered according to act of Congress, in the year 1881, by
CHAS. A. WIMER,
In the Office of the Librarian of Congress at Washington.

PREFACE.

This volume is the result of a careful compilation of the official record kept in President Garfield's case, and is issued in the present form (without any additions in the nature of historical or other incidental information) in order that it may preserve in its entirety a complete compendium of the official utterances of the physicians in charge of the case; thus making it an authentic reference-book for the medical profession and general reader.

The grateful acknowledgments of the compiler are extended to Mr. J. Stanley Brown, Private Secretary to the late President Garfield, for the material aid he has so courteously afforded, and through whose coöperation the early publication of this volume is rendered possible.

THE COMPILER.

OFFICIAL BULLETINS.

Executive Mansion.
July 2, 1881.

12 M.

The President is somewhat restless, but is suffering less pain. Pulse 112. Some nausea and vomiting have recently occurred. Considerable hemorrhage has taken place from the wound.

D. W. BLISS.

Executive Mansion.
July 2, 1881.

12.35 P. M.

The reaction from the shock of the injury has been very gradual. He is suffering some pain, but it is thought best not to disturb him by making any exploration for the ball until after the consultation at 3 P. M.

D. W. BLISS.

Executive Mansion.
July 2, 1881.

4 P. M.

President's condition is now somewhat less favorable. Evidences of internal hemorrhage being distinctly recognized.

Pulse, 130; temperature of body, 96.8°, which is a little below normal.

President suffers rather more pain, but mind is perfectly clear.

D. W. BLISS.

Executive Mansion,
July 2, 1881.

6 P. M.

The President has slept a few moments, but is manifestly weaker. Pulse 140, and feeble.

He is mentally clear, conversing intelligently when permitted to do so.

D. W. BLISS.

Executive Mansion,
July 3, 1881.

1 A. M.

The improvement in the President's condition, which began early in the evening, has steadily continued up to this hour.

His temperature and respiration are now normal, and his pulse has fallen to 120. The attending physicians regard all his symptoms as favorable, and a more hopeful feeling prevails.

D. W. BLISS.

Executive Mansion,
July 3, 1881.

10 A. M.

The President has rested quietly, and awakened refreshed; and his improving condition gives additional hope of his gradual recovery. Pulse, 114; respiration, 18; and temperature about normal.

D. W. BLISS.

Executive Mansion,
July 3, 1881.

11 A. M.

The President's condition is greatly improved. He secures sufficient refreshing sleep, and during his waking hours is cheerful, and is inclined to discuss pleasant topics. Pulse, 106, with more full and soft expression; temperature and respiration normal.

D. W. BLISS.

Executive Mansion,
July 3, 1881.

2 P. M.

The President has slept a good deal since last bulletin, though occasionally suffering from pain in both feet and ankles.

Pulse, 104; respiration, 18; temperature nearly normal. Whilst the President is by no means out of danger, yet his symptoms continue favorable.

D. W. BLISS.

Executive Mansion,
July 3, 1881.

6 P. M.

There is no appreciable change since the last bulletin. The President sleeps well at intervals. Pulse, 108; temperature and respiration normal.

D. W. BLISS,
J. K. BARNES,
J. J. WOODWARD.

Executive Mansion,
July 3, 1881.

10.30 o'clock P. M.

The condition of the President is less favorable. Pulse, 120; temperature, 100°; respiration, 20. He is more restless, and again complains of the pain in his feet.

D. W. BLISS.
J. K. BARNES,
J. J. WOODWARD,
ROBERT REYBURN.

EXECUTIVE MANSION,
July 4, 1881.

12.30 A. M.

The President's condition has changed very little since the last bulletin. Pulse, 112; temperature, 99.8°; respiration, 20. Some tympanites is recognized. Does not complain so much of pain in the feet.

D. W. BLISS,
J. K. BARNES,
J. J. WOODWARD,
ROBT. REYBURN.

In view of the fact that it is deemed best to keep the President perfectly quiet during the night, no further examinations will be made and no other bulletins issued until 7.30 this morning.

EXECUTIVE MANSION,
July 4, 1881.

8.15 A. M.

The condition of the President is not materially different from that reported in the last bulletin. He has dozed at intervals during the night, and at times has continued to complain of the pain in his feet.

The tympanites reported has not sensibly increased.

Pulse, 108; temperature, 99.4°; respiration, 19.

D. W. BLISS,
J. K. BARNES,
J. J. WOODWARD,
ROBERT REYBURN,
FRANK H. HAMILTON,
D. HAYES AGNEW.

Executive Mansion,
July 4, 1881.

7.45 P. M.

The President this evening is not so comfortable. He does not suffer so much from pain in the feet. The tympanites is again more noticeable. Pulse, 126; temperature, 101.9°; respiration, 24.

Another bulletin will be issued at 10 P. M., after which, in order not to distrub the President unnecessarily, no further bulletin will be issued till to-morrow morning.

D. W. BLISS,
J. J. WOODWARD,
J. K. BARNES,
ROBT. REYBURN.

Executive Mansion,
12.30 P. M.   July 5, 1881.

The favorable condition of the symptoms reported in the last bulletin continues. There has been no recurrence of the vomiting. Pulse, 110; temperature, 101°; respiration, 24.

The President lies at present in a natural sleep.

No further bulletin will be issued till 8.30 P. M., unless in case of an unfavorable change.

D. W. BLISS,
J. K. BARNES,
J. J. WOODWARD,
ROBT. REYBURN.

Executive Mansion,
8.30 P. M.   July 5, 1881.

The condition of the President continues as favorable as at the last bulletin. Pulse, 106; temperature 100.9°; respiration, 24.

No further bulletin will be issued till to-morrow morning, unless in case of unfavorable change.

D. W. BLISS,
J. K. BARNES.
J. J. WOODWARD,
ROBERT REYBURN.

Executive Mansion,
July 6, 1881.
8.30 A. M.

The President has passed a most comfortable night, and has slept well. His condition has remained throughout as favorable as when the last bulletin was issued. The pulse is becoming less frequent, and is now 98; temperature, 98.9°; respiration, 23.

D. W. BLISS,
J. K. BARNES,
J. J. WOODWARD,
ROBT. REYBURN.

The next bulletin will be issued at 12 o'clock M.

Executive Mansion,
12.30 P. M.   July 6, 1881.

The President remains quite as comfortable as at the date of the last bulletin. He takes his nourishment well. Pulse, 100; temperature, 99.7°; respiration, 23.

D. W. BLISS,
J. K. BARNES,
J. J. WOODWARD,
ROBT. REYBURN.

Unless unfavorable symptoms develop no further bulletins will be issued till 8.30 this evening.

Executive Mansion,
8.30 P. M.   July 6, 1881.

The President's condition continues as favorable as at last report. He has passed a very comfortable day, taking more nourishment than yesterday. Pulse, 104; temperature, 100.6°; respiration, 23.

D. W. BLISS,
J. K. BARNES,
J. J. WOODWARD,
ROBERT REYBURN.

No further bulletin will be issued to-night unless the conditions become unfavorable.

Executive Mansion,
July 7, 1881.
9 a. m.

The President has passed a most comfortable night, and continues steadily to improve. He is cheerful, and asks for additional food. Pulse, 94; temperature, 99.1°; respiration, 23.

D. W. BLISS,
J. K. BARNES,
J. J. WOODWARD,
ROBT. REYBURN.

The next bulletin will be issued at 1 o'clock p. m.

Executive Mansion,
July 7, 1881.
1 p. m.

The condition of the President continues quite as favorable as this morning. Pulse, 100; temperature, 100.8°; respiration, 23.

D. W. BLISS,
J. K. BARNES,
J. J. WOODWARD,
ROBERT REYBURN.

The next bulletin will be issued at 8.30 p. m.

Executive Mansion,
July 7, 1881.
8 p. m.

The favorable condition of the President continues. Pulse, 106; temperature, 100.2°; respiration, 23.

D. W. BLISS,
J. K. BARNES,
J. J. WOODWARD,
ROBERT REYBURN.

Unless unfavorable symptoms appear no further bulletin will be issued until to-morrow morning.

EXECUTIVE MANSION,
July 8, 1881.

8.15 A. M.

The condition of the President continues favorable. He is more comfortable than on any previous morning. Pulse, 96; temperature 99.2°; respiration, 23. The wound is beginning to discharge laudable pus.

D. W. BLISS,
J. K. BARNES,
J. J. WOODWARD,
ROBT. REYBURN.

The next bulletin will be issued at 1 o'clock P. M.

EXECUTIVE MANSION,
July 8, 1881.

12.30 P. M.

The progress of the President's case continues to be favorable. Pulse, 108; temperature 101.4°; respiration 24.

D. W. BLISS,
J. K. BARNES.
J. J. WOODWARD,
ROBT. REYBURN.

The President's condition continues so favorable that no further bulletin will be issued until 8.30 P. M.

EXECUTIVE MANSION,
July 8, 1881.

8. P. M.

The President's condition continues favorable. He has passed a very comfortable afternoon, and has taken more nutriment than on previous days. Pulse, 108; temperature 101.3°; respiration 24.

D. W. BLISS,
J. K. BARNES,
J. J. WOODWARD,
ROBT. REYBURN.

The conditions continue so favorable there will be no further bulletin until to-morrow morning.

Executive Mansion,
July 9, 1881.
8.30 A. M.

The President has passed a tranquil night, and this morning expresses himself as feeling quite comfortable. We regard the general progress of his case as very satisfactory. Pulse this morning, 100; temperature 99.4°; respiration 24.

D. W BLISS,
J. K. BARNES,
J. J. WOODWARD,
ROBT. REYBURN.

The next bulletin will be issued at 1 P. M.

Executive Mansion,
July 9, 1881.
1 P. M.

The condition of the President continues to be favorable. Pulse, 104; temperature, 101.2°; respiration, 22.

D. W. BLISS,
J. J. WOODWARD,
J. K. BARNES,
ROBT. REYBURN.

The next bulletin will be issued at 8.30 P. M.

Executive Mansion,
July 9, 1881.
7.30 P. M.

The President's condition has continued favorable during the day. The febrile reaction this afternoon does not differ materially from that of yesterday. Pulse, 108; temperature, 101.9°; respiration, 24.

D. W. BLISS,
J. K. BARNES,
J. J. WOODWARD,
ROBT. REYBURN.

The conditions are so favorable no further bulletin will be issued until to-morrow morning.

EXECUTIVE MANSION,
July 10, 1881.

8 A. M.

The President has passed the most comfortable night he has experienced since he was wounded, sleeping tranquilly and with few breaks. The general progress of his symptoms continues to be favorable. Pulse 106; temperature, 100°; respiration, 23.

D. W. BLISS,
J. K. BARNES,
J. J. WOODWARD,
ROBERT REYBURN.

The next bulletin will be issued at one.

EXECUTIVE MANSION,
July 10, 1881.

1 P. M.

The President's symptoms continue to be favorable. Pulse, 102; temperature, 100.5°; respiration, 22.

D. W. BLISS,
J. K. BARNES,
J. J. WOODWARD,
ROBT. REYBURN.

The next bulletin will be issued at 8.30 P. M.

EXECUTIVE MANSION,
July 10, 1881.

7 P. M.

The President's symptoms continue to make favorable progress. Pulse, 108; temperature, 101.9°; respiration, 24.

D. W. BLISS,
J. K. BARNES,
J. J. WOODWARD,
ROBT. REYBURN.

No further bulletin will be issued until to-morrow morning.

Executive Mansion,
July 11, 1881.

8 A. M.

The President has passed a comfortable night, and his condition shows an improvement over that of yesterday. Pulse, 98; temperature, 99.2°; respiration, 22.

D. W. BLISS,
J. K. BARNES,
J. J. WOODWARD,
ROBT. REYBURN.

Bulletins will be issued daily at 8 A. M., 1 P. M., and 8.30 P. M., until further notice.

Executive Mansion,
July 11, 1881.

1 P. M.

The favorable progress of the President's case continues. Pulse, 106; temperature, 99.8°; respiration, 24.

D. W. BLISS,
J. K. BARNES,
J. J. WOODWARD,
ROBT. REYBURN.

Executive Mansion,
July 11, 1881.

7 P. M.

The President has had rather more fever this afternoon; in other respects his condition is unchanged. Pulse, 108; temperature, 102.8°; respiration, 24.

D. W. BLISS,
J. K. BARNES,
J. J. WOODWARD,
ROBT. REYBURN.

EXECUTIVE MANSION,
July 12, 1881.

8 A. M.

The President is comfortable this morning. The rise of temperature noted in last evening's bulletin began to diminish about an hour later.

Pulse, 96 ; temperature, 99.6°; respiration, 22.

D. W. BLISS,
J. K. BARNES,
J. J. WOODWARD,
ROBT. REYBURN.

EXECUTIVE MANSION,
July 12, 1881.

1 P. M.

The President is passing a comfortable day. Pulse, 100 ; temperature, 100.8°: respiration, 24.

D. W. BLISS,
J. K. BARNES,
J. J. WOODWARD,
ROBT. REYBURN.

EXECUTIVE MANSION,
July 12, 1881.

7 P. M.

The President has passed a more comfortable day than yesterday.

Pulse, 104 ; temperature, 102.4°; respiration, 24.

D. W. BLISS,
J. K. BARNES,
J. J. WOODWARD,
ROBT. REYBURN.

EXECUTIVE MANSION,
July 13, 1881.

8.30 A M.

The President is doing well this morning. Pulse, 90; temperature, 98.5°; respiration, 20. His gradual progress towards recovery is manifest, and thus far without serious complications.

D. W. BLISS,
J. K. BARNES,
J. J. WOODWARD.
ROBT. REYBURN.

EXECUTIVE MANSION,
July 13, 1881.

1 P. M.

The President's condition continues favorable. Pulse, 94; temperature, 100.6°; respiration, 22.

D. W. BLISS,
J. K. BARNES,
J. J. WOODWARD,
ROBT. REYBURN.

EXECUTIVE MANSION,
July 13, 1881.

7 P. M.

The President has had less fever this afternoon than either yesterday or the day before. He continues slowly to improve. Pulse, 100 : temperature, 101.6°; respiration, 24.

D. W. BLISS,
J. K. BARNES,
J. J. WOODWARD,
ROBT. REYBURN.

EXECUTIVE MANSION,
July 14, 1881.

8.30 A. M.

The President has passed a comfortable night, and continues to do well. Pulse, 90; temperature, 99.8°; respiration, 22.

D. W. BLISS,
J. K. BARNES,
J. J. WOODWARD,
ROBT. REYBURN.

EXECUTIVE MANSION,
July 14, 1881.

1 P. M.

The progress of the President's case continues to be satisfactory this morning. Pulse, 94; temperature, 98.5°; respiration, 22.

D. W. BLISS,
J. K. BARNES,
J. J. WOODWARD.
ROBT. REYBURN.

EXECUTIVE MANSION,
July 14, 1881.

7 P. M.

The febrile rise this afternoon has been less pronounced, and has not caused the President so much discomfort. His general condition is good. Pulse, 98; temperature, 101°; respiration, 23.

D. W. BLISS,
J. K. BARNES,
J. J. WOODWARD,
ROBT. REYBURN.

Executive Mansion,
July 15, 1881.

8.30 a. m.

The President has rested well during the night, is doing admirably this morning, and takes his food with relish. Pulse, 90; temperature, 98.5°; respiration, 18.

D. W. BLISS,
J. K. BARNES,
J. J. WOODWARD.
ROBT. REYBURN.

Executive Mansion,
July 15, 1881.

1 p. m.

The President continues to do very well this morning. Pulse, 94; temperature, 98.5°; respiration, 18.

D. W. BLISS,
J. K. BARNES,
J. J. WOODWARD,
ROBT. REYBURN.

Executive Mansion,
July 15, 1881.

7 p. m.

The President has continued to do well during the day. The afternoon fever has been slighter than on any day since the 3d. Pulse, 98; temperature, 100.4°; respiration, 20.

D. W. BLISS,
J. K. BARNES,
J. J. WOODWARD,
ROBT. REYBURN.

EXECUTIVE MANSION,
July 16, 1881.

8.30 A. M.

The President has passed another good night, and is steadily progressing toward convalescence. Pulse, 90; temperature, 98.5°; respiration, 18.

D. W. BLISS,
J. K. BARNES,
J. J. WOODWARD,
ROBT. REYBURN.

In view of the favorable progress of the President's case, the surgeons have decided to issue bulletins hereafter only in the morning and evening.

EXECUTIVE MANSION,
July 16, 1881.

7 P. M.

The President has passed a better day than any since he was hurt. The afternoon fever is still less than yesterday. At 1 P. M. his pulse was 94; temperature, 98.4°; respiration, 18. His pulse is now 98; temperature, 100.2°; respiration, 19.

D. W. BLISS,
J. K. BARNES,
J. J. WOODWARD,
ROBT. REYBURN.

EXECUTIVE MANSION,
July 17, 1881.

8.30 A. M.

The President continues to improve. He passed an excellent night, and has a good appetite this morning. Pulse, 90; temperature, 98.4°; respiration, 18.

D. W. BLISS,
J. K. BARNES,
J. J. WOODWARD,
ROBERT REYBURN.

EXECUTIVE MANSION,
July 17, 1881.

7 P. M.

Our expectations of favorable progress have been fully realized by the manner in which the President has passed the day. He has taken more solid food, and with greater relish than hitherto, and his afternoon fever, which is as slight as that of yesterday, came on later. At 1 P. M. his pulse was 94, temperature, 98.5°; respiration, 18. At present, pulse, 98; temperature, 100.2°; respiration, 20.

D. W. BLISS,
J. K. BARNES,
J. J. WOODWARD,
ROBT. REYBURN.

EXECUTIVE MANSION,
July 18, 1881.

8.30 A. M.

The President has passed another comfortable night, and is doing well this morning. Pulse, 88; temperature, 98.4°; respiration, 18.

D. W. BLISS,
J. K. BARNES,
J. J. WOODWARD,
ROBT. REYBURN.

EXECUTIVE MANSION,
July 18, 1881.

7 P. M.

The President has had a little more fever this afternoon, which is regarded as merely a temporary fluctuation. At 1 P. M. his pulse was 98; temperature, 98.5°; respiration, 18. At present his pulse is 102; temperature, 100.7°; respiration, 21.

D. W. BLISS,
J. K. BARNES,
J. J. WOODWARD,
ROBT. REYBURN.

EXECUTIVE MANSION,
July 19, 1881.

8.30 A. M.

The President has passed a very good night, and this morning he is free from fever and expresses himself as feeling quite comfortable.

Pulse, 90 ; temperature, 98.5°; respiration, 18.

D. W. BLISS,
J. K. BARNES,
J. J. WOODWARD,
ROBT. REYBURN.

EXECUTIVE MANSION,
July 19, 1881.

7 P. M.

The President has passed an excellent day, and the afternoon fever has been less than on any day since he was wounded.

At 1 P. M. his pulse was 92 ; temperature, 98.5°; respiration, 19. At present his pulse is 96 ; temperature, 99.8°; respiration, 19.

D. W. BLISS,
J. K. BARNES,
J. J. WOODWARD,
ROBT. REYBURN.

EXECUTIVE MANSION,
July 20, 1881.

8.30 A. M.

The progress of the President towards recovery continues uninterruptedly. He has passed a quiet night.

Pulse this morning 86 ; temperature, 98.4°; respiration, 18.

D. W. BLISS,
J. K. BARNES,
J. J WOODWARD,
ROBT. REYBURN.

EXECUTIVE MANSION,
July 20, 1881.

7 P. M.

The President has passed an excellent day. At 1 P. M. his pulse was 88; temperature 98.4°; respiration, 18. At the present time his pulse is 98; temperature, 99.6°; respiration, 19.

D. W. BLISS,
J. K. BARNES,
J. J. WOODWARD,
ROBT. REYBURN.

EXECUTIVE MANSION,
July 21, 1881.

8.30 A. M.

The President has had a good night, and is doing excellently this morning. Pulse, 88; temperature, 98.4°; respiration, 18.

D. W. BLISS,
J. K. BARNES,
J. J. WOODWARD,
ROBERT REYBURN.

EXECUTIVE MANSION,
July 21, 1881.

7 P. M.

The President has had another good day. At 1 P. M. his pulse was 92; temperature, 98.4°; respiration, 19.
At 7 P. M.: pulse, 96; temperature, 99.9°; respiration, 19.

D. W. BLISS,
J. K. BARNES,
J. J. WOODWARD,
ROBT. REYBURN.

Executive Mansion,
July 22, 1881.

8.30 A. M.

The President rested well during the night, and is quite easy this morning. Pulse, 88; temperature, 98.4°; respiration, 17.

D. W. BLISS,
J. K. BARNES,
J. J. WOODWARD,
ROBT. REYBURN.

Executive Mansion,
July 22, 1881.

7.30 P. M.

The progress of the President's case continues without material change. At 1 P. M. his pulse was 98; temperature, 98.4°; respiration, 18.

At 7 P. M., pulse, 98; temperature, 100.2°; respiration, 19.

D. W. BLISS,
J. K. BARNES,
J. J. WOODWARD,
ROBT. REYBURN.

Executive Mansion,
July 23, 1881.

10 A. M.

The President was more restless last night, but this morning at 7 o'clock, while preparations were made to dress his wound, his temperature was found to be normal. Pulse, 92; temperature, 98.4°; respiration, 19.

At 7.30 he had a slight rigor, in consequence of which the dressing of his wound was postponed. Reaction followed promptly, and the dressing has now just been completed. At present his pulse is 110; temperature, 101°; respiration, 24.

D. W. BLISS,
J. K. BARNES,
J. J. WOODWARD,
ROBT. REYBURN.

EXECUTIVE MANSION,
July 23, 1881.

7 P. M.

After the bulletin of 10 A. M. the President's fever continued. At 11.30 A. M. he had again a slight rigor, and his temperature subsequently rose until, at 12.30 P. M., it was 104°; pulse, 125; respiration, 26. Between this time and 1 P. M. perspiration made its appearance, and the temperature began to fall gradually. It is now 101.7°; pulse, 118; respiration, 25. There has been a free discharge of pus from the wound during the day.

D. W. BLISS,
J. K. BARNES,
J. J. WOODWARD,
ROBT. REYBURN.

EXECUTIVE MANSION,
July 24, 1881.

8.30 A. M.

The President was more restless than usual during the night, and had another rigor just before midnight. This morning, at 8.15, his pulse was 98; temperature, 98.4°; respiration, 18. A consultation was then held with Dr. Hamilton, of New York, and Dr. Agnew, of Philadelphia, after which a counter-opening was made through the integument of the back, about three inches below the wound, which, it is hoped, will facilitate the drainage of pus and increase the chances of recovery. The President bore the operation well, and his pulse is now 112.

D. W. BLISS,
J. K. BARNES,
J. J. WOODWARD,
ROBT. REYBURN.

EXECUTIVE MANSION,
July 24, 1881.

7 P. M.

The President has been much relieved by the operation of this morning, and the pus has been discharging satisfactory through the new opening. At noon to-day his pulse was 118; temperature, 99.8°; respiration, 24. At present his pulse is 104; temperature, 99.2°; respiration, 23.

D. W. BLISS,
J. K. BARNES,
J. J. WOODWARD,
ROBT. REYBURN.

EXECUTIVE MANSION,
July 25, 1881.

8.30 A. M.

The President has passed a more comfortable night, and has had no rigor since that reported in the bulletin of yesterday morning. He is doing well this morning. Pulse, 96; temperature, 98.4°; respiration, 18.

D. W. BLISS,
J. K. BARNES,
J. J. WOODWARD,
ROBT. REYBURN.

EXECUTIVE MANSION,
July 25, 1881.

7 P. M.

The President has done well during the day. His afternoon fever did not come on until after three o'clock. It is somewhat higher than yesterday, but there has been no chill. At noon his pulse was 104; temperature, 98.4°; respiration 20. At 7 P. M. his pulse was 110; temperature 101.8°; respiration, 24.

D. W. BLISS,
J. K. BARNES,
J. J. WOODWARD,
ROBT. REYBURN.

Executive Mansion,
July 26, 1881.

8.30 A. M.

The President was somewhat restless during the night, and the fever, which had subsided after our last bulletin, rose again about midnight and continued until 3 A. M., after which it again subsided. He is now about as well as yesterday at the same hour. Pulse, 102; temperature, 98.4°; respiration, 18.

D. W. BLISS,
J. K. BARNES,
J. J. WOODWARD,
ROBT. REYBURN.

Executive Mansion,
July 26, 1881.

7 P. M.

The President has done well during the day. At the dressing of the wound, after the morning bulletin was issued, a displaced spiculum of the broken rib about half an inch long was removed; the track of the wound at this point was dilated and a larger drainage tube inserted, for the purpose of facilitating the discharge of pus. Since that time he has had several quiet naps, has taken more nourishment than on any of the last five days, without gastric irritation, and when the wound was dressed this evening the discharge of healthy pus was satisfactorily abundant. At noon his pulse was 106; temperature 98.4°; respiration 19. At 7 P. M., pulse, 104; temperature 100.7°; respiration 22.

D. W. BLISS,
J. K. BARNES,
J. J. WOODWARD,
ROBT. REYBURN,
D. HAYES AGNEW.

EXECUTIVE MANSION.
July 27, 1881.

8 A. M.

The President slept sweetly last night from about 8 P. M. to 5 A. M., with but a single break of short duration at 11 P. M. Since 5 o'clock this morning he has dozed quietly, awakening at intervals. There have been no rigors. He takes his nourishment well, and his general condition is improving. He expresses himself as feeling better and more rested. Pulse, 94; temperature 98.4°; respiration 18.

D. W. BLISS,
J. K. BARNES,
J. J. WOODWARD,
ROBT. REYBURN,
D. HAYES AGNEW.

EXECUTIVE MANSION,
July 27, 1881.

12.30 P. M.

The President's wound was dressed just after the morning bulletin was issued. It looks well, and the pus, which is healthy in character, is discharging freely. Since then he has rested quietly, and takes his nourishment readily and without gastric disturbance.

At present his pulse is 90; temperature 98.4°; respiration 18.

D. W. BLISS,
J K. BARNES,
J. J. WOODWARD,
ROBT. REYBURN.

Executive Mansion,
July 27, 1881.

7 p. m.

The President is still resting quietly. He has been able to take more nourishment to day than for several days past, and up to the present hour has had no febrile rise of temperature. His wound has just been dressed. It looks well and has continued to discharge healthy pus in sufficient quantity during the day.

His pulse, is now 96; temperature 98.5°; respiration 20.

D. W. BLISS,
J. K. BARNES,
J. J. WOODWARD,
ROBT. REYBURN.

Executive Mansion,
July 28, 1881.

8 a. m.

The President rested well during the night and no rigor or febrile disturbance has occured since the bulletin of yesterday evening. This morning the improvement of his general condition is distinctly perceptible. He appears refreshed by the night's rest, and expresses himself cheerfully as to his condition. Pulse, 92; temperature 98.4°; respiration 18.

FRANK H. HAMILTON,
D. W. BLISS,
J. K. BARNES,
J. J. WOODWARD,
ROBT. REYBURN.

EXECUTIVE MANSION,
July 28, 1881.

12.30 P. M.

The President bore the dressing of his wound this morning with less fatigue than hitherto. It appears well, and is discharging sufficiently. Shortly afterwards his bed was rolled into an adjoining room while that occupied till now is being throughly cleansed and put in order. His pulse is now 94 ; temperature 98.5°; respiration 18.

FRANK H. HAMILTON,
D. W. BLISS,
J. K. BARNES,
J. J. WOODWARD,
ROBT. REYBURN.

EXECUTIVE MANSION,
July 28, 1881.

7 P. M.

The President has passed a pleasant day, and has taken his nourishment with apparent relish. His temperature continued normal until about 5 o'clock, when a moderate afternoon rise occurred, which, however, gives the patient but slight discomfort, and causes no anxiety. At present his pulse is 104 ; temperature, 100.5°; respiration, 20.

FRANK H. HAMILTON,
D. W. BLISS,
J. K. BARNES,
J. J. WOODWARD,
ROBT. REYBURN.

Executive Mansion,
July 29, 1881.

8.30 A. M.

Immediately after the evening dressing yesterday the President's afternoon fever began gradually to subside. He slept well during the night, and this morning is free from fever, looks well, and expresses himself cheerfully. No rigors have occurred during the past twenty-four hours, nor indeed at any time since the 25th instant. A moderate rise of temperature in the afternoon is to be anticipated for some days to come. At present his pulse is 92; temperature, 98.4°; respiration, 18.

FRANK H. HAMILTON,
D. W. BLISS,
J. K. BARNES,
J. J. WOODWARD,
ROBT. REYBURN.

Executive Mansion,
July 29, 1881.

12.30 P. M.

The President bore the dressing of his wound well this morning, and exhibited very little fatigue after its completion. The appearance of the wound, the character and quantity of the discharge, and the general condition of the patient are satisfactory. He rests well and takes an adequate quantity of nourishment. At present his pulse is 98; temperature, 98.4°; respiration, 19.

FRANK H. HAMILTON,
D. W. BLISS,
J. K. BARNES,
J. J. WOODWARD,
ROBT. REYBURN.

EXECUTIVE MANSION,
July 29, 1881.

7 P. M.

The President has been comfortable and cheerful during the day, and has had quite a nap since the noon bulletin was issued. The afternoon febrile rise came on later, and was not so marked as yesterday. The wound has been discharging freely and looks well. At present his pulse is 98; temperature, 100°; respiration, 20.

FRANK H. HAMILTON,
D. W. BLISS,
J. K. BARNES,
J. J. WOODWARD,
ROBT. REYBURN.

EXECUTIVE MANSION,
July 30, 1881.

8.30 A. M.

The President enjoyed a refreshing sleep during the greater part of the night. The slight febrile rise of yesterday afternoon had subsided by midnight, and this morning his temperature is again normal. A gradual improvement of his general condition, in all particulars, is observable, and is recognized by himself. His pulse is now 92; temperature, 98.5°; respiration, 18.

FRANK H. HAMILTON,
D. W. BLISS,
J. K. BARNES,
J. J. WOODWARD,
ROBT. REYBURN.

EXECUTIVE MANSION,
July 30, 1881.

12.30 P. M.

The President showed no fatigue from the dressing of his wound this morning. It looks very well, and the discharge of pus is satisfactory in quantity and quality. His general condition continues gradually to improve. A moderate quantity of solid food has been added to his nourishment, and was eaten with relish. A frame has been introduced beneath the mattress of his bed by which his head and shoulders have been elevated somewhat, and he expresses himself as well pleased with the change of position. At present his pulse is 98; temperature, 98.5°; respiration, 20.

FRANK H. HAMILTON,
D. W. BLISS,
J. K. BARNES,
J. J. WOODWARD,
ROBT. REYBURN.

EXECUTIVE MANSION,
July 30, 1881.

7 P. M.

The President has passed the day comfortably without drawback or unpleasant symptoms, and has taken an ample amount of nourishment. The afternoon rise of temperature is moderate, and did not commence until about five o'clock. The discharge of pus has been abundant, and at the evening dressing was washed away freely from the deeper parts of the wound. At present his pulse is 104; temperature, 100.2°; respiration, 20.

FRANK H. HAMILTON,   D. W. BLISS,
D. HAYES AGNEW.   J. K. BARNES,
                     J. J. WOODWARD,
                     ROBT. REYBURN.

Executive Mansion,
July 31, 1881.

8.30 A. M.

The President slept well during the night, and awoke refreshed this morning. The afternoon fever subsided earlier than the night before, and had quite disappeared by 10 P. M. His appearance and expressions this morning indicate continued improvement. At present his pulse is 94; temperature, 98.4°; respiration, 18.

D. W. BLISS,
J. K. BARNES,
J. J. WOODWARD,
ROBT. REYBURN,
D. HAYES AGNEW.

Executive Mansion.
July 31, 1881.

12.30 P. M.

The President bore the morning dressing of his wound without fatigue. It continues to look well and discharge adequately. After the wound was dressed he ate, with relish, a breakfast of solid food, and has since passed a comfortable morning, during which he had a pleasant nap. The quantity of nourishment now taken daily is regarded as quite sufficient to support his system and favor the gradual increase in strength, which is plainly observable. At present his pulse is 100; temperature, 98.5°; respiration, 19.

D. HAYES AGNEW. D. W. BLISS,
J. K. BARNES,
J. J. WOODWARD,
ROBT. REYBURN.

Executive Mansion,
July 31, 1881.

7 P. M.

The President has passed an excellent day. From just after the morning dressing till about 6 P. M. he has had his head and shoulders elevated by a frame beneath the mattress ; he has taken and relished an ample supply of nourishment, and continues to improve in general condition. The appearance of the wound at the evening dressing was in every way satisfactory. The afternoon rise of temperature has been quite insignificant. At present his pulse is 104 : temperature, 99°; respiration, 20.

D. HAYES AGNEW.   D. W. BLISS,
J. K. BARNES,
J. J. WOODWARD,
ROBT. REYBURN.

Executive Mansion,
August 1, 1881.

8.30 A. M.

The President slept well during the night, and this morning is cheerful and expresses himself as feeling better than at any time since he was hurt. After the slight rise of yesterday afternoon his temperature became again normal early in the evening, and so continued. He appears stronger and has evidently made good progress on the road towards recovery during the last few days. His pulse is now 94 ; temperature, 98.4° ; respiration, 18.

D. HAYES AGNEW,
D. W. BLISS,
J. K. BARNES,
J. J. WOODWARD,
ROBERT REYBURN.

EXECUTIVE MANSION,
August 1, 1881.

12.30 P. M.

The President's wound continues to do well. At the morning dressing it was found to be in all respects in a satisfactory condition. After the dressing was concluded his head and shoulders were raised in the same manner as yesterday, and he took solid food for breakfast with more relish than he has hitherto shown. At present his pulse is 100; temperature, 98.4°; respiration, 19.

D. HAYES AGNEW.   D. W. BLISS,
J. K. BARNES,
J. J. WOODWARD,
ROBT. REYBURN.

EXECUTIVE MANSION,
August 1, 1881.

7 P. M.

The President remained with his head and shoulders elevated until time for dressing his wound this evening. It continues to progress in a satisfactory manner and discharges healthy pus freely from the deeper as well as the superficial portions. He has taken nourishment well and in sufficient quantity, and in all respects continues to do well. The rise of temperature this afternoon is slight. At present his pulse is 104; temperature, 99.5°; respiration 20.

D. HAYES AGNEW.   D. W. BLISS,
J. K. BARNES,
J. J. WOODWARD,
ROBT. REYBURN.

EXECUTIVE MANSION,
August 2, 1881.

8.30 A. M.

The President passed a very pleasant night and slept sweetly the greater part of the time. This morning he awoke refreshed and appears comfortable and cheerful. Pulse, 94; temperature, 98.4°: respiration, 18.

D. W. BLISS,
J. K. BARNES,
J. J. WOODWARD,
ROBT. REYBURN,
D. HAYES AGNEW.

EXECUTIVE MANSION,
August 2, 1881.

12.30 P. M.

The President is passing the day comfortably with his head and shoulders raised in the same manner as yesterday. At the morning dressing his wound was found to be doing admirably. His pulse is now 99; temperature, 98.4°; respiration, 19.

D. HAYES AGNEW.

D. W. BLISS,
J. K. BARNES,
J. J. WOODWARD,
ROBT. REYBURN.

EXECUTIVE MANSION,
August 2, 1881.

7 P. M.

The President has continued to progress favorably during the day, and appears perceptibly better in his general condition than yesterday, a more natural tone of voice being especially perceptible. The appearance of the external wounds, at the evening dresssing, was exceedingly good; that made by the ball is rapidly granulating, while the discharge from the deeper portion of the wound, which is abundant and healthy, comes through the counter opening made by operation. The rise of temperature this afternoon is moderate and attended by no inconvenience to the patient. At present his pulse is 104 ; temperature, 100° ; respiration ; 20.

D. HAYES AGNEW. D. W. BLISS,
J. K. BARNES,
J. J. WOODWARD,
ROBT. REYBURN.

EXECUTIVE MANSION,
August 3, 1881.
8.30 A. M.

The President slept tranquilly the greater part of the night. This morning his temperature is normal, and his general condition is satisfactory. Another day of favorable progress is anticipated. At present his pulse is 96 ; temperature 98.4° ; respiration, 18.

D. HAYES AGNEW. D. W. BLISS,
J. K. BARNES,
J. J. WOODWARD,
ROBT. REYBURN.

EXECUTIVE MANSION,
August 3, 1881.
12.30 P. M.

The President continues to progress steadily towards convalescence. He has taken to-day an increased proportion of solid food, his wound is doing well, and his general condition is better than yesterday. At present his pulse is 100 ; temperature, 98.4° ; respiration, 19.

D. W. BLISS,
J. K. BARNES,
J. J. WOODWARD,
ROBT. REYBURN.

EXECUTIVE MANSION,
August 3, 1881.

7 P. M.

The President has passed a very satisfactory day. The wound continues to do well; he takes an adequate quantity of nourishment, and appears in all respects better than at any time since he was injured. The rise of temperature this afternoon is slight. At present his pulse is 102; temperature, 99.4°; respiration, 19.

D. W. BLISS,
J. K. BARNES,
J. J. WOODWARD,
ROBT. REYBURN.

EXECUTIVE MANSION,
August 4, 1881.

8.30 A. M.

The President continues to improve. He slept well during the night, and this morning looks and expresses himself cheerfully. Another satisfactory day is anticipated. At present his pulse is 90; temperature, 98.4°; respiration, 18.

The next bulletin will be issued this evening, and hereafter the noon bulletin will be dispensed with.

FRANK H. HAMILTON.   D. W. BLISS,
J. K. BARNES,
J. J. WOODWARD,
ROBT. REYBURN.

Executive Mansion,
August 4, 1881.

7 P. M.

As the morning bulletin indicated would probably be the case, the President has passed another good day, without drawback or unpleasant symptom of any kind. He has taken his nourishment well, and shown little fatigue after his dressings and changes of position. The wound is doing well both in appearance and in the character and amount of discharge. At 12.30 P. M. his pulse was 96; temperature, 98.4°; respiration, 18. The afternoon rise of temperature came on late and was moderate in degree. At 7 P. M. his pulse is 102; temperature, 100.2°; respiration, 19.

FRANK H. HAMILTON.   D. W. BLISS,
                                       J. K. BARNES,
                                       J. J. WOODWARD,
                                       ROBT. REYBURN.

Executive Mansion,
August 5, 1881.

8.30 A. M.

The President slept naturally the greater part of the night, although he has taken no morphia during the last twenty-four hours. His improved condition warranted, several days ago, a diminution in the quantity of morphia administered hypodermically at bed time, and it was reduced at first to $\frac{1}{12}$ and afterwards to $\frac{1}{16}$ of a grain in the twenty-four hours, without any consequent unpleasant result, and finally has been altogether dispensed with. His condition this morning exhibits continued improvement, and another good day is anticipated.

At present his pulse is 88; temperature, 98.4°; respiration, 18.

FRANK H. HAMILTON.   D. W. BLISS,
                                       J. K. BARNES,
                                       J. J. WOODWARD,
                                       ROBT. REYBURN.

EXECUTIVE MANSION,
August 5, 1881.

7 P. M.

The President has passed another good day. The appearance of the wound and the character and amount of the discharge of pus continues satisfactory. He has taken an adequate quantity of nourishment, and has had several pleasant naps during the day. At 12.30 P. M. his pulse was 98; temperature, 98.4°; respiration, 18. After 4 P. M. his temperature began to rise as usual, but to a moderate degree, and without perceptible dryness of skin. At present his pulse is 102; temperature, 100.4°; respiration, 19.

FRANK H. HAMILTON.   D. W. BLISS,
J. K. BARNES,
J. J. WOODWARD,
ROBT. REYBURN.

———

EXECUTIVE MANSION,
August 6, 1881.

8.30 A. M.

The President has passed an excellent night, sleeping sweetly the greater part of the time without the aid of morphia or any other anodyne. This morning he is cheerful and all the indications promise another favorable day. Pulse, 92; temperature, 98.4°; respiration, 18.

D. W. BLISS,
J. K. BARNES,
J. J. WOODWARD,
ROBT. REYBURN,
FRANK H. HAMILTON.

7 P. M.

EXECUTIVE MANSION,
August 6, 1881.

The President passed a comfortable morning, his symptoms and general condition being quite satisfactory. At 12.30 P. M. his pulse was 100; temperature, 98.5°; respiration, 19. During the afternoon he complained somewhat of the weather. The external heat being such that it was found impracticable to keep the temperature of his room much below 90°, without closing the windows and doors, which was not thought prudent. The afternoon rise of his temperature began as late as yesterday, but has been higher, though unaccompanied by dryness of skin. At 7 P. M. his pulse was 102; temperature, 101.8°; respiration, 19. The appearance of the wound at the evening dressing was, however, good, and there has been no interruption to the flow of pus.

FRANK H. HAMILTON. D. W. BLISS,
J. K. BARNES,
J. J. WOODWARD,
ROBT. REYBURN.

8.30 A. M.

EXECUTIVE MANSION,
August 7, 1881.

Shortly after the bulletin of last evening was issued the President fell into a pleasant sleep, during which the febrile rise subsided, and was no longer perceptible when he awoke at 10 P. M. Subsequently he slept well, though with occasional breaks during the rest of the night. No morphia or other anodyne was administered. This morning he is in good condition, although the effects of the febrile disturbance of yesterday are still slightly perceptible in pulse and temperature. At present his pulse is 96; temperature, 98.7°; respiration, 18.

FRANK H. HAMILTON, D. W. BLISS.
D. HAYES AGNEW. J. K. BARNES,
J. J. WOODWARD,
ROBT. REYBURN.

Executive Mansion,

August 7, 1881.

7 p. m.

The President has been comfortable during the day, although his temperature began to rise earlier than yesterday, and rose almost as high. At 12.30 p. m. his pulse was 104'; temperature, 100°; respiration, 20   At 7 p. m. his pulse is 104 ; temperature, 101.2°; respiration, 20 ; nevertheless, he has been able to take nourishment as usual ; has had several refreshing naps during the day.   The discharge of pus has been liberal and is healthy in character.

FRANK H. HAMILTON,   D. W. BLISS,
D. HAYES AGNEW.   J. K. BARNES,
                                    J. J. WOODWARD,
                                    ROBT. REYBURN.

Executive Mansion,
August 8, 1881.

8.30 a. m.

The President passed a comfortable night, and slept well without anodyne. The rise of temperature of yesterday afternoon subsided during the evening, and did not recur at any time through the night. At present he appears better than yesterday morning. Pulse, 94 ; temperature, 98.4°; respiration, 18.

FRANK H. HAMILTON,   D. W. BLISS,
D. HAYES AGNEW.   J. K. BARNES,
                                    J. J. WOODWARD,
                                    ROBT. REYBURN.

Executive Mansion,
August 8, 1881.

10.30 A. M.

It having become necessary to make a further opening to facilitate the escape of pus, we took advantage of the improved condition of the President this morning. Shortly after the morning bulletin was issued he was etherized, the incision extending downward and forward, and a counter-opening made into the track of the ball below the margin of the twelfth rib, which, it is believed, will effect the desired object. He bore the operation well, and has now recovered from the effects of etherization, and is in excellent condition.

FRANK H. HAMILTON,
D. HAYES AGNEW.

D. W. BLISS,
J. K. BARNES,
J. J. WOODWARD,
ROBT. REYBURN.

Executive Mansion,
August 8, 1881.

7 P. M.

After the last bulletin was issued the President suffered somewhat for a time from nausea due to the ether, but this has now subsided. He has had several refreshing naps, and his general condition is even better than might have been expected after the etherization and operation. At noon his pulse was 104; temperature, 100.2°; respiration, 20. At present his pulse is 108; temperature, 101.9°; respiration, 19. Under the circumstances the fever must be regarded as moderate.

D. HAYES AGNEW.

D. W. BLISS,
J. K. BARNES,
J. J. WOODWARD,
ROBT. REYBURN.

Executive Mansion,
August 9, 1881.

8.30 A. M.

Notwithstanding the effects of yesterday's operation the President slept the greater part of the night without the use of any anodyne. The febrile rise of yesterday afternoon slowly subsided during the night. This morning at 8.30 his pulse is 98; temperature, 99.8°; respiration, 19. Since yesterday afternoon small quantities of liquid nourishment, given at short intervals, have been retained, and this morning larger quantities are being administered without gastric disturbance.

D. HAYES AGNEW.   D. W. BLISS,
                              J. K. BARNES,
                              J. J. WOODWARD,
                              ROBT. REYBURN.

Executive Mansion,
August 9, 1881.

12.30 P. M.

At the dressing of the President's wound this morning it was found that pus had been discharging spontaneously and freely through the counter-opening made yesterday. He has been quite comfortable this morning and taken a liberal supply of liquid nourishment. His pulse is now 104; temperature, 99.7°; respiration, 19.

D. HAYES AGNEW.   D. W. BLISS,
                              J. K. BARNES,
                              J. J. WOODWARD,
                              ROBT. REYBURN.

EXECUTIVE MANSION,
7 P. M. *August* 9, 1881.

The President has been easy during the day, and has continued to take the nourishment allowed, without gastric disturbances. The discharge of pus from his wound is quite abundant, and it is evident that thorough drainage has been secured by yesterday's operation. The degree of fever this afternoon differs little from that of yesterday. Pulse, 106; temperature, 101.9°; respiration, 19.

D. W. BLISS,
J. K. BARNES,
J. J. WOODWARD,
ROBT. REYBURN.

EXECUTIVE MANSION,
8 A. M. *August* 10, 1881.

The President slept soundly during the night, and this morning his temperature is again normal, although his pulse is still frequent. At present it is 104; temperature, 98.5°; respiration, 19.

D. W. BLISS,
J. K. BARNES,
J. J. WOODWARD,
ROBT. REYBURN.

EXECUTIVE MANSION,
12.30 P. M. *August* 10, 1881.

The President is getting through the day in a very satisfactory manner. He has asked for and taken a small quantity of solid food in addition to the liquid nourishment allowed. At the morning dressing the discharge of pus through the new opening was more free than at any previous time; its character was good, and the wound looks well. His temperature and respiration continue within the normal range, though the debility following the operation is still shown by frequency of pulse. At present his pulse is 100; temperature, 98.6°; respiration, 19.

D. W. BLISS,
J. K. BARNES,
J. J. WOODWARD,
ROBT. REYBURN.

Executive Mansion,
August 10, 1881.

7 P. M.

The President has passed an excellent day. The drainage of the wound is now efficient, and the pus secreted by its deeper portions has been coming away spontaneously. The afternoon rise of temperature is almost a degree less than yesterday and the day before. Pulse at present, 108; temperature, 101°; respiration, 19.

D. W. BLISS,
J. K. BARNES,
J. J. WOODWARD,
ROBT. REYBURN.

Executive Mansion,
August 11, 1881.

8.30 A. M.

The President has passed an exceedingly good night, sleeping sweetly, with but few short breaks, and awaking refreshed this morning, at a later hour than usual. At the morning dressing, just completed, it was found that the deeper parts of the wound had been emptied spontaneously. The quantity of pus secreted is beginning to diminish; its character and the appearance of the wound are healthy. His temperature shows an entire absence of fever this morning, and his pulse, which is less frequent than yesterday, is improving in quality. At present it is 100; temperature 98.6°; respiration, 19.

D. W. BLISS,
J. K. BARNES,
J. J. WOODWARD,
ROBT. REYBURN.

EXECUTIVE MANSION,
August 11, 1881.

12.30 P. M.

The President is doing very well to-day. Besides a liberal supply of liquid nourishment at regular intervals, he has taken for breakfast, with evident relish, an increased quantity of solid food. He continues free from fever, his skin moist, but without undue perspiration. Pulse, 102; temperature, 98.6°; respiration, 19.

D. W. BLISS,
J. K. BARNES,
J. J. WOODWARD,
ROBT. REYBURN.

EXECUTIVE MANSION,
August 11, 1881.

7 P. M.

After the noon bulletin was issued the President's condition continued as then reported until about 4 P. M., when the commencement of the afternoon febrile rise was noted. In its degree it did not differ materially from that of yesterday. His pulse is now 108; temperature, 101.2°; respiration, 19.

D. W. BLISS,
J. K. BARNES,
J. J. WOODWARD,
ROBT. REYBURN.

EXECUTIVE MANSION,
August 12, 1881.

8.30 A. M.

The President slept well the greater part of the night. The fever of yesterday afternoon subsided during the evening, and has not been perceptible since 10 P. M. His general condition this morning is good. Pulse, 100; temperature, 98.6°; respiration, 19.

D. W. BLISS,
J. K. BARNES,
J. J. WOODWARD,
ROBERT REYBURN,
FRANK H. HAMILTON.

Executive Mansion.
August 12, 1881.

12.30 p. m.

The President has passed a comfortable morning. He continues to take, without repugnance, the liquid nourishment allowed, and ate, with relish, for breakfast a larger quantity of solid food than he took yesterday. At present his pulse is 100 ; temperature 99.3°; respiration 19.

FRANK H. HAMILTON.   D. W. BLISS,
J. K. BARNES,
J. J. WOODWARD,
ROBT. REYBURN.

Executive Mansion,
August 12, 1881.

7 p. m.

The President has passed a comfortable day. At the evening dressing the wound was found to be doing well. The quantity of pus secreted is gradually diminishing ; its character is healthy. The rise of temperature this afternoon reached the same point as yesterday. At present the pulse is 108 ; temperature 101.2°; respiration 19.

FRANK H. HAMILTON.   D. W. BLISS,
J. K. BARNES,
J. J. WOODWARD,
ROBT. REYBURN.

Executive Mansion,
August 13, 1881.

8.30 a. m.

The President did not sleep as well as usual during the early part of last night. After midnight, however, his sleep was refreshing, and only broken at long intervals. This morning he has a little fever, nevertheless he expresses himself as feeling better than for several days past. Pulse 104 ; temperature 100.8°; respiration 19.

FRANK H. HAMILTON.   D. W. BLISS,
J. K. BARNES,
J. J. WOODWARD,
ROBT. REYBURN.

Executive Mansion,
August 13, 1881.
12.30 P. M.

The President has been cheerful and easy during the morning, and his temperature has fallen a little more than a degree and a half since the morning bulletin was issued. The wound is discharging healthy pus. His pulse is now 102; temperature 99.2°; respiration 18.

FRANK H. HAMILTON.   D. W. BLISS,
J. K. BARNES,
J. J. WOODWARD,
ROBT. REYBURN.

Executive Mansion,
August 13, 1881.
6.30 P. M.

Since the last bulletin the President has continued to do well. The afternoon fever has been half a degree less than yesterday. At the evening dressing the appearance of the wound was improved. The discharge of pus has been adequate, and its character is healthy. At present his pulse is 104; temperature, 100.7°; respiration 19.

FRANK H. HAMILTON.   D. W. BLISS,
J. K. BARNES,
J. J. WOODWARD,
ROBT. REYBURN.

Executive Mansion,
August 14, 1881.
8.30 A. M.

The President slept well during the night, and this morning expresses himself as feeling comfortable. His temperature is one degree less than at the same hour yesterday. His general condition is good. Pulse, 100; temperature, 99.8°; respiration 18.

D. W. BLISS,
J. K. BARNES,
J. J. WOODWARD,
ROBT. REYBURN.

EXECUTIVE MANSION,
August 14, 1881.

12.30 P. M.

The President has done well this morning; his temperature falling half a degree since the last bulletin was issued. At the morning dressing the condition of the wound was found to be excellent, and the discharge of pus adequate and healthy. Pulse, 96; temperature, 99.3°; respiration, 18.

D. HAYES AGNEW.   D. W. BLISS,
J. K. BARNES,
J. J. WOODWARD,
ROBT. REYBURN.

EXECUTIVE MANSION,
August 14, 1881.

6.30 P. M.

The condition of the President has not materially changed since noon. The afternoon febrile rise is about the same as yesterday. Pulse, 108; temperature, 100.8°; respiration, 19.

D. HAYES AGNEW.   D. W. BLISS,
J. K. BARNES,
J. J. WOODWARD,
ROBT. REYBURN,

EXECUTIVE MANSION,
August 15, 1881.

8.30 A. M.

The President did not rest as well as usual last night. Until towards three o'clock his sleep was not sound, and he awoke at short intervals. His stomach was irritable and he vomited several times. About three o'clock he became composed and slept well until after seven this morning. His stomach is still irritable, and his temperature rather higher than yesterday morning. At present his pulse is 108; temperature, 100.2°; respiration, 20.

D. HAYES AGNEW.   D. W. BLISS,
J. K. BARNES,
J. J. WOODWARD,
ROBT. REYBURN.

Executive Mansion,
August 15, 1881.

12.30 p. m.

Since the last bulletin the President has not again vomited, and has been able to retain the nourishment administered. At the morning dressing the discharge of pus was free and of good character. Since then his pulse has been more frequent, but the temperature has fallen to a little below what it was at this time yesterday. At present his pulse is 118, temperature, 99°; respiration, 19.

D. HAYES AGNEW,   D. W. BLISS,
                        J. K. BARNES,
                        J. J. WOODWARD,
                        ROBT. REYBURN.

———

Executive Mansion,
August 15, 1881.

6.30 p. m.

The irritability of the President's stomach returned during the afternoon, and he has vomited three times since one o'clock. Although the afternoon rise of temperature is less than it has been for several days, the pulse and respiration are more frequent, so that his condition is, on the whole, less satisfactory. His pulse is now 130; temperature, 99.6°; respiration, 22.

D. HAYES AGNEW,   D. W. BLISS,
                        J. K. BARNES,
                        J. J. WOODWARD,
                        ROBT. REYBURN.

8.30 A. M.   EXECUTIVE MANSION,
                                        August 16, 1881.

The President was somewhat restless and vomited several times during the early part of the night. Since three o'clock this morning he has not vomited, and has slept tranquilly most of the time. Nutritious enemata are successfully employed to sustain him. Altogether the symptoms appear less urgent than yesterday afternoon. At present his pulse is 110 ; temperature, 98.6° ; respiration, 18.

                                   D. W. BLISS,
                                   J. K. BARNES,
                                   J. J. WOODWARD,
                                   ROBT. REYBURN,
                                   D. HAYES AGNEW.

12.30 P. M.   EXECUTIVE MANSION,
                                       August 16, 1881.

The President has been tranquil, and has not vomitted since the morning bulletin, but has not yet rallied from the prostration of yesterday afternoon as much as was hoped. The enemata administered are, however, still retained. At present his pulse is 114 ; temperature, 98.3° ; resperation, 18.

D. HAYES AGNEW.   D. W. BLISS,
                                   J. K. BARNES,
                                   J. J. WOODWARD,
                                   ROBT. REYBURN.

7 P. M.   EXECUTIVE MANSION,
                                       August 16, 1881.

The President's symptoms are still grave, yet he seems to have lost no ground during the day, and his condition on the whole is rather better than yesterday. He has vomited but once during the afternoon; the enemata are retained. At present his pulse is 120 ; temperature, 98.9°; respiration, 19.

D. HAYES AGNEW.   D. W. BLISS,
                                   J. K. BARNES,
                                   J. J. WOODWARD,
                                   ROBT. REYBURN.

8.30 A. M.

EXECUTIVE MANSION,
August 17, 1881.

The President has passed a tranquil night, sleeping most of the time. He continues to retain the nutritive enemata, and has not vomited since the last bulletin. His general condition appears more hopeful than this time yesterday. Pulse, 110; temperature, 98.3°; respiration, 18.

FRANK H. HAMILTON,
D. HAYES AGNEW.
D. W. BLISS,
J. K. BARNES,
J. J. WOODWARD,
ROBT. REYBURN.

12.30 P. M.

EXECUTIVE MANSION,
August 17, 1881.

The President's condition has not materially changed since the last bulletin. He has been tranquil and has slept some; has not vomited, and the nutritive enemata are still retained. Pulse, 112; temperature, 98.7°; respiration, 18.

FRANK H. HAMILTON,
D. HAYES AGNEW.
D. W. BLISS,
J. K. BARNES,
J. J. WOODWARD,
ROBT. REYBURN.

6.30 P. M.

EXECUTIVE MANSION,
August 17, 1881.

The President's condition is even better than it was this morning. There has been no vomiting during the day, and the enamata continue to be retained. Moreover, a teaspoonful of beef extract has twice been administered by the mouth and not rejected, and small quantities of water swallowed from time to time excite no nausea. The wound continues to do well.

At present his pulse is 112; temperature, 98.8; respiration, 18.

FRANK H. HAMILTON,
D. HAYES AGNEW.
D. W. BLISS,
J. K. BARNES,
J. J. WOODWARD,
ROBT. REYBURN.

Executive Mansion,
August 18, 1881.

8.30 A. M.

The President has passed a very comfortable night, sleeping well the greater part of the time. There has been no further vomiting, and the nutritive enemata are still retained. This morning his pulse is slower and his general condition better than yesterday at the same hour.

Pulse, 104; temperature, 98.8°; respiration, 17.

FRANK H. HAMILTON,   D. W. BLISS,
D. HAYES AGNEW.   J. K. BARNES,
                                J. J. WOODWARD,
                                ROBT. REYBURN.

Executive Mansion,
August 18, 1881.

12.30 P. M.

The President is suffering some discomfort this morning from commencing inflammation of the right parotid gland. In other respects, his condition is somewhat improved, and especially his stomach is becoming less intolerant. He has asked for and retained several portions of liquid nourishment, much more than he could swallow yesterday. The nutritive enemata continue to be used with success.

At present his pulse is 108; temperature, 98.4°; respiration, 18.

FRANK H. HAMILTON.   D. W. BLISS,
                                J. K. BARNES,
                                J. J. WOODWARD,
                                ROBT. REYBURN.

6.30 P. M.   EXECUTIVE MANSION,
                                                      August 18, 1881.

The President has done well during the day. He has taken additional nourishment by the mouth this afternoon, with evident relish, and without subsequent nausea. There is some rise of temperature, but his general condition is rather better than this time yesterday. Pulse, 108; temperature, 100; respiration, 18.

FRANK H. HAMILTON.   D. W. BLISS,
                                      J. K. BARNES,
                                      J. J. WOODWARD,
                                      ROBT. REYBURN.

                                      EXECUTIVE MANSION.
8.30 A. M.   August 19, 1881.

The President slept much of the night, and this morning is more comfortable than yesterday. The swelling of the right parotid gland has not increased since yesterday afternoon, and he is now free from pain. Nutritive enemata are still given with success, and liquid food has already this morning been swallowed and relished. Pulse, 100; temperature, 98.4°; respiration, 17.

FRANK H. HAMILTON.   D. W. BLISS,
                                      J. K. BARNES,
                                      J. J. WOODWARD,
                                      ROBT. REYBURN.

                                      EXECUTIVE MANSION.
12.30 P. M.   August 19, 1881.

The President's condition has perceptibly improved during the last twenty-four hours. The parotid swelling is evidently diminishing, and it has not pained him since last night. He is taking to-day an increased quantity of liquid food by the mouth, which is relished, and produces no gastric irritation. His pulse is now 106; temperature, 98.8°; respiration, 17.

FRANK H. HAMILTON.   D. W. BLISS,
                                      J. K. BARNES.
                                      J. J. WOODWARD,
                                      ROBT. REYBURN.

EXECUTIVE MANSION,
August 19, 1881.

6.30 P. M.

The President has been easy during the afternoon, and the favorable conditions reported in the last bulletin continue. The swollen parotid gland has not been painful. The temperature is the same; the pulse rather less frequent than at this hour yesterday. Pulse, 106; temperature, 100°; respiration, 18.

D. W. BLISS,
J. K. BARNES,
J. J. WOODWARD,
ROBT. REYBURN.

EXECUTIVE MANSION,
August 20, 1881.

8.30 A. M.

The President has passed a quiet night, and this morning his condition does not differ materially from what it was yesterday at the same hour. The swelling of the parotid gland is unchanged and is free from pain. This morning his pulse is 98; temperature, 98.4°; respiration, 18.

D. HAYES AGNEW,   D. W. BLISS,
J. K. BARNES,
J. J. WOODWARD,
ROBT. REYBURN.

EXECUTIVE MANSION,
August 20, 1881.

12.30 P. M.

The President continues to do well. He is taking liquid food by the mouth in increased quantity and with relish. The nutritive enemata are still successfully given, but at longer intervals. His pulse is now 107; temperature, 98.4°; respiration, 18. At the morning dressing the wound was looking well and the pus discharged was of healthy character. After the operation of August 8, the flexible tube used to wash out the wound at each dressing readily followed the track of the ball to the depth of three and a half or four inches. At the dressing, however, a small quantity of healthy pus came, as was believed, from the part of the track beyond this point, either spontaneously or after gentle pressure over the anterior surface of the right iliac region; but this deeper part of the track was not reached by the tube until yesterday morning, when the separation of a small slough permitted it to pass, unresisted, downward and forward for the distance of twelve and a half inches from the external surface of the last incision. This facilitates the drainage and cleansing of the deeper parts of the wound, but has not been followed by any increase in the quantity of pus discharged. The large pus cavity which had formed in the immediate vicinty of the broken rib is filling up with healthy granulations, and the original wound of entrance, as far as that cavity, has healed.

D. HAYES AGNEW.   D. W. BLISS,
  J. K. BARNES,
  J. J. WOODWARD,
  ROBT. REYBURN.

Executive Mansion,
August 20, 1881.

6.30 P. M.

The President has passed the day quietly. He has been able to take more liquid food by the mouth than yesterday, and the quantity given by enema has been proportionally diminished. The parotid swelling remains about the same. Pulse, 110; temperature, 100°; respiration, 19.

D. HAYES AGNEW.   D. W. BLISS,
  J. K. BARNES,
  J. J. WOODWARD,
  ROBT. REYBURN.

8.30 a. m.   Executive Mansion.
             August 21, 1881.

The President awoke more frequently than usual, yet slept sufficiently during the night, and appears comfortable this morning. The parotid swelling is about the same, but is not painful. He took liquid nourishment by the mouth several times during the night, as well as this morning. Pulse, 106; temperature, 98.8°; respiration, 18.

D. HAYES AGNEW.   D. W. BLISS,
                       J. K. BARNES,
                       J. J. WOODWARD,
                       ROBT. REYBURN.

                       Executive Mansion,
12.30 p. m.   *August* 21, 1881.

The President's condition continues about as at the morning bulletin, except that there is a slight rise of temperature. He continues to take liquid nourishment by the mouth as well as by enema. Pulse, 108; temperature, 99.4°; respiration, 18.

D. HAYES AGNEW.   D. W. BLISS,
                       J. K. BARNES,
                       J. J. WOODWARD,
                       ROBT. REYBURN.

                       Executive Mansion,
6.30 p. m.   *August* 21, 1881.

The President has vomited twice during the afternoon. The administration of food by the mouth has therefore again been temporarily suspended, and the nutritive enemata will be given more frequently. His temperature is lower and his pulse rather less frequent than yesterday afternoon. The parotid swelling is painless, but stationary. Pulse, 108; temperature, 99.2°; respiration, 18.

D. HAYES AGNEW.   D. W. BLISS,
                       J. K. BARNES,
                       J. J. WOODWARD,
                       ROBT. REYBURN.

EXECUTIVE MANSION,
August 22, 1881.

8.30 A. M.

The President has not vomited since yesterday afternoon, and this morning has twice asked for and received a small quantity of fluid nourishment by the mouth. He slept more quietly during the night, and this morning his general condition is more encouraging than when the last bulletin was issued.

Pulse, 104; temperature, 98.4°; respiration, 18.

D. HAYES AGNEW.   D. W. BLISS,
J. K. BARNES.
J. J. WOODWARD,
ROBT. REYBURN.

EXECUTIVE MANSION,
August 22, 1881.

12.30 P. M.

The President has continued this morning to retain liquid nourishment taken by the mouth, as well as by enema. There has been no recurrence of the vomiting and no nausea. The parotid swelling is not materially smaller, but continues painless. It has caused, for a day or two, an annoying accumulation of viscid mucus in the back of the mouth, but this symptom has now much abated.

At present his pulse is 104; temperature, 98.4°; respiration, 18.

D. HAYES AGNEW.   D. W. BLISS,
J. K. BARNES,
J. J. WOODWARD,
ROBT. REYBURN.

EXECUTIVE MANSION,
August 22, 1881.

6.30 P. M.

The President has continued to take liquid nourishment in small quantities at stated intervals during the entire day, and has had no return of nausea or vomiting. The nutritive enemata are also retained. The wound is looking well, and the work of repair is going on in all portions exposed to view. The pus discharge is healthy. Pulse, 110; temperature, 100.1°; respiration, 19.

D. W. BLISS,
J. K. BARNES,
J. J. WOODWARD,
ROBT. REYBURN,
D. HAYES AGNEW.

EXECUTIVE MANSION,
August 23, 1881.

8.30 A. M.

The President slept the greater part of the night, but awoke at frequent intervals. He has taken, since last evening, a larger quantity of liquid food by the mouth than in the corresponding hours of any day during the past week. The use of nutrient enemata is continued at longer intervals. The parotid swelling is unchanged. Pulse, 100; temperature, 98.4°; respiration, 18.

D. W. BLISS,
J. K. BARNES,
J. J. WOODWARD,
ROBT. REYBURN,
D. HAYES AGNEW.

EXECUTIVE MANSION,
August 23, 1881.

12.30 P. M.

The President continues to take by the mouth and retain an increased quantity of liquid food. At the morning dressing the wound looked well, and the pus was of healthy character. The mucus accumulations in the back of the mouth, on account of the parotid swelling, is less viscid, and now gives but little trouble. At present his pulse is 104; temperature, 98.9°; respiration, 18.

D. W. BLISS,
J. K. BARNES,
J. J. WOODWARD,
ROBT. REYBURN.

EXECUTIVE MANSION,
August 23, 1881.

6.30 P. M.

The President has continued to take liquid food by the mouth at regular intervals during the day, and has had no recurrence of gastric disorder. The parotid swelling remains unchanged; in other respects, the symptoms show some improvement over his condition yesterday afternoon. Pulse, 104; temperature, 99.2°; respiration, 19.

D. W. BLISS,
J. K. BARNES,
J. J. WOODWARD.
ROBT. REYBURN.

Executive Mansion.
August 24, 1881.

8.30 A. M.

The President has passed a very good night, awakening at longer intervals than during several nights past. He continues to take liquid food by the mouth with more relish and in such quantity that the enemata will be suspended for the present. No change has yet been observed in the parotid swelling; the other symptoms are quite as favorable as yesterday.

Pulse, 100; temperature, 98.5°; respiration, 17.

FRANK H. HAMILTON.   D. W. BLISS,
                                  J. K. BARNES,
                                  J. J. WOODWARD,
                                  ROBT. REYBURN.

Executive Mansion,
August 24, 1881.

12.30 P. M.

The President continues to take liquid food by the mouth, as reported in the last bulletin. His temperature has risen slightly since that time; in other respects, his condition is about the same.

Pulse, 104; temperature, 99.2°; respiration, 17.

FRANK H. HAMILTON.   D. W. BLISS,
                                  J. K. BARNES,
                                  J. J. WOODWARD,
                                  ROBT. REYBURN.

EXECUTIVE MANSION,
August 24, 1881.

6. 30 P. M.

Shortly after the noon bulletin was issued an incision was made into the swelling on the right side of the President's face, for the purpose of relieving the tension of the swollen parotid gland and of giving vent to pus, a small quantity of which was evacuated. He has taken a larger quantity of liquid food by the mouth to-day than yesterday, and has been entirely free from nausea. His temperature this afternoon is, however, higher than yesterday at the same hour, and his pulse somewhat more frequent.

Pulse, 108; temperature, 100.7°; respiration, 19.

FRANK H. HAMILTON.   D. W. BLISS,
                             J. K. BARNES,
                             J. J. WOODWARD,
                             ROBT. REYBURN.

EXECUTIVE MANSION,
August 25, 1881.

8.30 A. M.

The President slept most of the night. He has taken liquid food by the mouth at stated intervals and in sufficient quantity, so that the enemata have not been renewed. No modification of the parotid swelling has yet been observed. His general condition is much the same as at this time yesterday. Pulse, 106; temperature, 98.5°; respiration, 18.

D. HAYES AGNEW,   D. W. BLISS,
FRANK H. HAMILTON.   J. K. BARNES,
                             J. J. WOODWARD,
                             ROBT. REYBURN.

EXECUTIVE MANSION,
August 25, 1881.

9.15 A. M.

The subject of the removal of the President from Washington at the present time was earnestly considered by us last night and again this morning. After mature deliberation the conclusion was arrived at by the majority that it would not now be prudent, although all agree that it will be very desirable at the earliest time at which his condition may warrant it. We are moreover unanimously of the opinion that at no time since the injury has the President exhibited any symptoms of malaria.

FRANK H. HAMILTON, D. W. BLISS,
D. HAYES AGNEW.   J. K. BARNES,
          J. J. WOODWARD.
          ROBT. REYBURN.

EXECUTIVE MANSION,
August 25, 1881.

12.30 P. M.

Since the issue of this morning's bulletin a rise in the President's temperature, similar to that which occurred yesterday morning, has been observed. His pulse is somewhat more frequent. From the incision in the parotid swelling a few drops of pus were discharged this morning; the size of the swelling has not diminished. In other respects his condition has not perceptibly changed. Pulse, 112; temperature, 99.2°; respiration, 19.

FRANK H. HAMILTON.   D. W. BLISS,
          J. K. BARNES,
          J. J. WOODWARD,
          ROBT. REYBURN.

EXECUTIVE MANSION,
August 25, 1881.

6.30 P. M.

There has been little change in the President's condition since the noon bulletin was issued. The frequency of his pulse is now the same as then. His temperature has risen somewhat, but is not so high as yesterday evening. There has been a slight discharge of pus during the day from the incision in the parotid swelling, but it is not diminishing in size. No unfavorable change has been observed in the condition of the wound. He has taken by the mouth a sufficient supply of liquid food. At present his pulse is 112; temperature, 99.8°; respiration, 19.

FRANK H. HAMILTON.   D. W. BLISS,
                       J. K. BARNES,
                       J. J. WOODWARD,
                       ROBT. REYBURN.

EXECUTIVE MANSION,
August 26, 1881.

8.30 A. M.

The President slept most of the night, awakening at intervals of half an hour to an hour. On first awakening there was, as there has been for several nights past, some mental confusion, which disappeared when he was fully roused, and occasionally he muttered in his sleep. These symptoms have abated this morning as on previous days. At present his temperature is slightly above the normal and his pulse a little more frequent than yesterday morning. Pulse, 108; temperature, 99.1°; respiration, 17.

FRANK H. HAMILTON.   D. W. BLISS,
                       J. K. BARNES,
                       J. J. WOODWARD,
                       ROBT. REYBURN.

EXECUTIVE MANSION,
August 26, 1881.

12.30 P. M.

At the morning dressing of the President it was observed that pus from the parotid swelling had found its way spontaneously into his right external auditory meatus, through which it was discharging; some pus was also discharging through the incision made into the swelling. His wound looks as well as it has done for some time past. His pulse and temperature are at present higher than at the corresponding hour for some days. He continues to take by the mouth the liquid food prescribed, nevertheless we regard his condition as critical.

Pulse 118; temperature 100°; respiration 18.

FRANK H. HAMILTON.   D. W. BLISS,
J. K. BARNES,
J. J. WOODWARD,
ROBT. REYBURN.

EXECUTIVE MANSION,
August 26, 1881.

6.30 P. M.

The President's condition has not changed materially since the last bulletin was issued. He continues to take by the mouth the liquid food prescribed, and occasionally asks for it. Since yesterday forenoon, commencing at 11.30 A. M., the enemata have again been given at regular intervals, as a means of administering stimulants as well as nutrition. They are retained without trouble. At present his pulse is 116; temperature 99.9°; respiration 18.

FRANK H. HAMILTON.   D. W. BLISS,
J. K. BARNES,
J. J. WOODWARD,
ROBT. REYBURN.

Executive Mansion,
August 27, 1881.
8.30 A. M.

The President slept from half an hour to an hour, or more, at a time throughout the night. He continues to retain the liquid food administered by the mouth, and the stimulating enemata; nevertheless his pulse has been more frequent since midnight, and he is evidently feebler this morning than yesterday.

Pulse, 120; temperature 98.4^c; respiration 22.

FRANK H. HAMILTON.   D. W. BLISS,
J. K. BARNES,
J. J. WOODWARD,
ROBT. REYBURN.

Executive Mansion,
August 27, 1881.
12.30 P. M.

There has been no improvement in the President's condition, since the last bulletin was issued. He continues to retain the liquid food administered by the mouth as well as the enemata. At the morning dressing the parotid swelling appeared about the same as yesterday. No material change was observed in the wound. Since morning the temperature has risen about a degree, and the pulse has fluctuated somewhat. At present the pulse is 120; temperature 99.6^c; respiration 22.

FRANK H. HAMILTON.   D. W. BLISS,
J. K. BARNES,
J. J. WOODWARD,
ROBT. REYBURN.

EXECUTIVE MANSION,
August 27, 1881.

6.30 P. M.

The President's symptoms show slight amelioration this afternoon; his pulse is somewhat less frequent, and his temperature lower; moreover the mental disturbance described in yesterday morning's bulletin has disappeared. The parotid swelling has discharged a little pus by the opening spontaneously formed into the ear, as well as by the incision made, but is not perceptibly smaller. The liquid food given by the mouth, and the enemata continue to be retained.

Pulse, 114: temperature, 98.9°; respiraion, 22.

FRANK H. HAMILTON,   D. W. BLISS,
D. HAYES AGNEW.   J. K. BARNES,
   J. J. WOODWARD,
   ROBT. REYBURN.

EXECUTIVE MANSION,
August 28, 1881.

8.30 A. M.

The amelioration of the President's symptoms announced in last evening's bulletin continued during the night, and since midnight some further improvement has been observed, the pulse progressively diminishing in frequency. The stomach has continued to retain the liquid nourishment administered, and last evening he asked for, and ate, a small quantity of milk-toast. Stimulating and nutrient enemata continue to be retained. There has been no mental disturbance during the night or this morning. At present his pulse is 100; temperature, 98.4°; respiration, 17.

FRANK H. HAMILTON,   D. W. BLISS,
D. HAYES AGNEW.   J. K. BARNES,
   J. J. WOODWARD,
   ROBT. REYBURN.

EXECUTIVE MANSION,
August 28, 1881.
12.30 P. M.

At the morning dressing of the President several yellowish points were observed just below the ear over the swollen parotid, and an incision being made, about a teaspoonful of healthy looking pus escaped. There was also some discharge of pus through the two openings (into the ear and the incision) mentioned in previous bulletins. The wound looks rather less indolent than it has been doing for several days past. Since the morning bulletin there has been some rise of temperature, but little increase in the frequency of pulse, and in other respects no material change has occurred. Pulse, 104; temperature, 99.5°; respiration, 18.

FRANK H. HAMILTON.   D. W. BLISS.
D. HAYES AGNEW.   J. K. BARNES.
                                J. J. WOODWARD,
                                ROBT. REYBURN.

EXECUTIVE MANSION,
August 28, 1881.
6.30 P. M.

The improvement in the President's condition declared yesterday afternoon is still maintained. He continues to take willingly the liquid food given by the mouth, and is apparently digesting it. The stimulants and nutrients given by enema are also retained. At the evening dressing an increased quantity of healthy looking pus was discharged from the suppurating parotid. The appearance of the wound has not perceptibly changed since the morning dressing. But little rise in temperature or pulse has taken place since noon, and the pulse is perceptibly stronger than this time yesterday. Pulse, 110; temperature, 99.7°; respiration 20.

FRANK H. HAMILTON,   D. W. BLISS.
D. HAYES AGNEW.   J. K. BARNES,
                                J. J. WOODWARD,
                                ROBERT REYBURN.

EXECUTIVE MANSION,
August 29, 1881.

8.30 A M.

The President,s symptoms this morning are as favorable as yesterday at the same hour. He slept, awakening at intervals, the greater part of the night. At these intervals he took, and retained, the liquid nourishment administered. His mind continues perfectly clear. Pulse, 100; temperature, 98.5°; respiration, 17.

D. HAYES AGNEW.   D. W. BLISS.
J. K. BARNES,
J. J. WOODWARD,
ROBT. REYBURN.

EXECUTIVE MANSION,
August 29, 1881.

12.30 P. M.

At the morning dressing of the President an additional point of suppuration was recognized in his swollen face, which, being incised, gave exit to some healthy looking pus. The other openings on the exterior of the swelling are likewise discharging, but though less tense, the tumefaction has not yet materially diminished in size. Nothing new has been observed in the condition of the wound. The usual daily rise of temperature has not yet occurred, and the general condition has not materially changed since morning. Pulse. 106; temperature, 98.6°; respiration 18.

D. HAYES AGNEW.   D. W. BLISS,
J. K. BARNES.
J. J. WOODWARD,
ROBT. REYBURN.

Executive Mansion,
August 29, 1881.

6.30 P. M.

The daily rise of the President,s temperature began later this afternoon than yesterday, but rose eight-tenths of a degree higher. The frequency of his pulse is now the same as at this hour yesterday. He has taken willingly the liquid food prescribed during the day, and had besides, during the morning, a small piece of milk toast. At the evening dressing a pretty free discharge of healthy puss took place from the parotid swelling, which is perceptibly diminishing in size. The wound manifests no material change. Pulse, 110; temperature 100.5°; respiration, 18.

D. HAYES AGNEW.   D. W. BLISS,
　　　　　　　　　　J. K. BARNES,
　　　　　　　　　　J. J. WOODWARD,
　　　　　　　　　　ROBT. REYBURN.

Executive Mansion,
August 30, 1881.

8.30 A. M.

The President slept the greater part of the night, awaking at intervals, and retaining the liquid nourishment administered. His general condition this morning is about the same as at the same hour yesterday. Pulse, 102; temperature, 98.5°; respiration, 18.

D. HAYES AGNEW.   D. W. BLISS,
　　　　　　　　　　J. K. BARNES,
　　　　　　　　　　J. J. WOODWARD,
　　　　　　　　　　ROBT. REYBURN.

Executive Mansion,
August 30, 1881.

12.30 P. M.

At the morning dressing another small incision was made in the lower part of the swelling on the right side of the President's face, which was followed by a free discharge of healthy looking pus. A similar discharge took place through the other openings. The swelling is perceptibly smaller and looks better. The wound remains in an unchanged condition. There has been little rise of temperature since morning, but the pulse is more frequent. In other respects the condition is about the same. Pulse, 116; temperature, 98.9°; respiration, 18.

D. HAYES AGNEW.   D. W. BLISS,
                       J. K. BARNES,
                       J. J. WOODWARD,
                       ROBT. REYBURN.

Executive Mansion,
August 30, 1881.

6.30 P. M.

The President has passed comfortably through the day. He has taken the usual amount of nourishment by the mouth, with stimulating enemata at stated periods. His rise of temperature this afternoon is a degree less than yesterday at the same time, and his pulse is less frequent than at noon to-day. The parotid swelling has been discharging more freely, and is continuing to diminish in size. Pulse, 109; temperature, 99.5°; respiration, 18.

D. HAYES AGNEW.   D. W. BLISS,
                       J. K. BARNES,
                       J. J. WOODWARD,
                       ROBT. REYBURN.

EXECUTIVE MANSION,
August 31, 1881.
8.30 A. M.

The President has passed a tranquil night and this morning his condition is quite as favorable as yesterday at the same hour. Pulse, 100 ; temperature, 98.4° ; respiration, 18.

FRANK H. HAMILTON,   D. W. BLISS,
D. HAYES AGNEW.   J. K. BARNES,
                        J. J. WOODWARD,
                        ROBT. REYBURN.

EXECUTIVE MANSION,
August 31, 1881.
12.30 P. M.

At the dressing of the President this morning the parotid swelling was found to be discharging freely. It looks well, and has materially diminished in size. The wound remains in about the same state. His general condition is evidently more favorable than at this hour yesterday. Pulse, 95 ; temperature, 98.4°; respiration, 17.

FRANK H. HAMILTON,   D. W. BLISS,
D. HAYES AGNEW.   J. K. BARNES,
                        J. J. WOODWARD,
                        ROBT. REYBURN.

EXECUTIVE MANSION,
August 31, 1881.
6.30 P. M.

The President has passed a better day than for some time past. He has taken his food with increased relish, and the usual afternoon rise of temperature did not occur. At the evening dressing the fluid used to wash out the parotid abscess found its way into the mouth, which it did not do this morning, showing that an opening into the mouth has spontaneously occurred. The abscess is discharging freely, and the swelling continues to diminish. There is some increase in the discharge of pus from the wound. Pulse, 109; temperature, 98.6°; respiration, 18.

FRANK H. HAMILTON.   D. W. BLISS,
J. K. BARNES,
J. J. WOODWARD,
ROBT. REYBURN.

EXECUTIVE MANSION,
8.30 A. M.   *September* 1, 1881.

Towards nine o'clock last evening the President had some feverishness, and his pulse ranged from 108 to 116. This condition, which was unaccompanied by rigors or sweating, had subsided by midnight and did not interfere with his sleep. He had on the whole a good night, and this morning his condition is fully as favorable as yesterday at the same hour. Pulse, 100; temperature, 98.4°; respiration, 17.

FRANK H. HAMILTON.   D. W. BLISS,
J. K. BARNES,
J. J, WOODWARD,
ROBT. REYBURN.

EXECUTIVE MANSION,
12.30 P. M.   *September* 1, 1881.

At the morning dressing of the President the abscess of the parotid was found to be discharging freely. It looks well and continues to diminish in size. The state of the wound remains the same. His general condition is not materially different from what it was at this hour yesterday, except that the pulse is somewhat more frequent. Pulse, 108; temperature, 98.6°; respiration, 18.

FRANK H. HAMILTON.   D. W. BLISS,
J. K. BARNES,
J. J. WOODWARD,
ROBT. REYBURN.

Executive Mansion,
September 1, 1881.
6.30 P. M.

The condition of the President has not materially changed since the last bulletin, except that there has been a moderate rise of temperature this afternoon. It having been represented to us that a portion of this morning's bulletin has been misunderstood, we would state that the President has had no rigors for several weeks. At present his pulse is 108; temperature, 99.4°; respiration, 18.

FRANK H. HAMILTON.   D. W. BLISS,
J. K. BARNES,
J. J. WOODWARD,
ROBERT REYBURN.

Executive Mansion,
September 2, 1881.
8.30 A. M.

The President slept well during the night, and this morning his condition is, in all respects, as favorable as yesterday at the same hour.

Pulse, 100; temperature, 98.4°; respiration, 17.

FRANK H. HAMILTON.   D. W. BLISS,
J. K. BARNES,
J. J. WOODWARD,
ROBERT REYBURN.

Executive Mansion,
September 2, 1881.
12.30 P. M.

The President's condition has not materially changed since the morning bulletin was issued. Pulse, 100; temperature, 98.7°; respiration, 18.

FRANK H. HAMILTON.   D. W. BLISS,
J. K. BARNES,
J. J. WOODWARD,
ROBT. REYBURN.

Executive Mansion,
September 2, 1881.

6.30 p. m.

The President has passed a comfortable day, and this evening appears better than for some days past. He has taken a larger proportion of nutriment by the mouth and manifested greater relish for it. His pulse shows some improvement as regards frequency and strength. The parotid abscess continues to improve. The wound shows as yet little change. This evening his pulse is 104 ; temperature, 99.2°; respiration, 18.

FRANK H. HAMILTON.   D. W. BLISS,
J. K. BARNES,
J. J. WOODWARD,
ROBT. REYBURN.

Executive Mansion,
September 3, 1881.

8.30 a. m.

The President was somewhat more restless than usual during the early part of the night, but slept better after 1 a. m. This morning his general condition does not differ materially from what it was at the same hour yesterday, except that there is a slight increase in the frequency of the pulse.

Pulse, 104; temperature, 98.6°; respiration, 18.

FRANK H. HAMILTON.   D. W. BLISS,
J. K. BARNES,
J. J. WOODWARD,
ROBT. REYBURN.

EXECUTIVE MANSION,
September 3, 1881.
12.30 P. M.

The President's condition has not materially changed since the morning bulletin was issued. Pulse, 104; temperature, 98.4°; respiration, 18.

FRANK H. HAMILTON,
D. HAYES AGNEW.
D. W. BLISS,
J. K. BARNES,
J. J. WOODWARD,
ROBT. REYBURN.

EXECUTIVE MANSION,
September 3, 1881.
6.30 P. M.

The President has done well during the day, and has taken, with some relish, a sufficient quantity of nutriment. The parotid swelling continues to discharge freely and to diminish in size. The wound shows no material change. Altogether his general condition exhibits some improvement over yesterday. Pulse, 102; temperature, 99.6°; respiration, 18.

D. HAYES AGNEW.
D. W. BLISS,
J. K. BARNES,
J. J. WOODWARD,
ROBT. REYBURN.

EXECUTIVE MANSION,
September 4, 1881.
8.30 A. M.

The President vomited once late last evening, and once about an hour after midnight. Notwithstanding this disturbance he slept well most of the night, and this morning has taken food by the mouth without nausea, and has retained it. His pulse is somewhat more frequent, but in other respects his condition is about the same as at this hour yesterday.

Pulse, 108; temperature 98.4°; respiration, 18.

D. HAYES AGNEW.
D. W. BLISS,
J. K. BARNES,
J. J. WOODWARD,
ROBT. REYBURN.

EXECUTIVE MANSION,
September 4, 1881.

12.30 P. M.

The Presidents condition has not changed materially since the last bulletin was issued, and there has been no further gastric disturbance. Pulse, 106; temperature, 98.4°; respiration, 18.

D. HAYES AGNEW.   D. W. BLISS,
J. K. BARNES,
J. J. WOODWARD,
ROBT. REYBURN.

EXECUTIVE MANSION,
September 4, 1881.

6.30 P. M.

The President has passed a comfortable day. He has taken his food with some relish and had no return of the irritability of stomach reported in the morning's bulletin. The parotid swelling continues to improve, and is now so far reduced that the contour of his face is restored. The wound shows no material change. The rise of temperature this afternoon has been very slight, but his pulse was more frequent throughout the day than yesterday or the day before, and he showed more fatigue after the dressings. Pulse, 110; temperature, 99°; respiration, 18.

D. HAYES AGNEW.   D. W. BLISS,
J. K. BARNES,
J. J. WOODWARD,
ROBT. REYBURN.

Executive Mansion,
September 5, 1881.

8.30 A M.

The President was somewhat restless during the early part of the night, but slept well after midnight. He has taken by the mouth and retained the nutriment prescribed. This morning his pulse is less frequent than yesterday. His temperature is a degree above normal. Pulse, 102; temperature, 99.5; respiration, 18.

D. HAYES AGNEW.   D. W. BLISS,
J. K. BARNES,
J. J. WOODWARD,
ROBT. REYBURN.

Executive Mansion,
September 5, 1881.

12.30 P. M.

The President's condition has not changed materially since the last bulletin was issued, except that there is some increase in the frequency of the pulse. He has taken, with some relish, the nourishment administered by the mouth, and had no return of gastric irritability.

Pulse, 114; temperature, 99.5°; respiration, 18.

D. HAYES AGNEW.   D. W. BLISS,
J. K. BARNES,
J. J. WOODWARD,
ROBT. REYBURN.

EXECUTIVE MANSION,
September 5, 1881.

6.30 P. M.

No material change has taken place in the condition of the President since morning. The parotid abcess continues to improve, and the wound remains about the same. The pulse is somewhat less frequent than at noon. At present it is 108; temperature, 99.8°; respiration, 18. Should no untoward symptoms prevent, it is hoped to move the President to Long Branch to-morrow.

D. HAYES AGNEW. D. W. BLISS,
  J. K. BARNES,
  J. J. WOODWARD,
  ROBT. REYBURN.

LONG BRANCH, N. J.,
September 6, 1881.

6.30 P. M.

Since the last bulletin was issued the President has been removed from Washington to Long Branch. He was more restless than usual last night, being evidently somewhat excited by anticipations of the journey. This morning at 5.30 A. M. his pulse was 118; temperature, 99.8°; respiration, 18. We left Washington with the President at 6.30 A. M. Owing to the admirable arragements made by the Pennsylvania railroad company, and to the ingeniously-arranged bed, designed by Mr. T. N. Ely, the fatigue incident to the transportation was reduced to a minimum. Nevertheless, as was anticipated, some signs of the disturbance produced by the journey have been exhibited since his arrival, by rise of temperature and increased frequency of pulse. At present his pulse is 124; temperature, 101.6°; respiration 18.

FRANK H. HAMILTON, D. W. BLISS,
D. HAYES AGNEW. J. K. BARNES,
  J. J. WOODWARD,
  ROBT. REYBURN.

Elberon, N. J.,
September 7, 1881.

9 A. M.

The President slept the greater part of the night, awakening, however, as often as it was necessary to give nourishment, which he took very well. The fever reported in last evening's bulletin had subsided by 11 P. M. This morning his temperature is normal, and he appears to have quite recovered from the fatigue of yesterday's journey. At the morning dressing the parotid abscess was found to be doing well. The visible part of the wound looks somewhat better. Pulse, 106; temperature, 98.4°; respiration, 18.

The next bulletin will be issued at 6 o'clock this evening.

FRANK H. HAMILTON, D. W. BLISS,
D. HAYES AGNEW.   J. K. BARNES,
            J. J. WOODWARD,
            ROBT. REYBURN.

Elberon, N. J.,
September 7, 1881.

6 P. M.

Notwithstanding the exceptional heat of the the weather, [the thermometer in his bedroom rose to 94° at half-past three this afternoon,] there was a breeze most of the day, so that the President was comparatively comfortable. He has taken his nourishment regularly, and has slept at intervals during the day. At 12.15 P. M. his pulse was 114; temperature, 98.4°; respiration, 18. Since then there has been some rise of temperature, though less than yesterday, and the pulse has somewhat diminished in frequency. At the evening dressing the appearance of the wound was favorable. At present his pulse is 108; temperature, 101°; respiration, 18.

FRANK H. HAMILTON,   D. W. BLISS,
            J. K. BARNES,
            J. J. WOODWARD,
            ROBT. REYBURN.

ELBERON, N. J.,
September 8, 1881.

8.30 A. M.

At the morning examination made at 8 o'clock, the President's pulse was 104; temperature, 98.7°, and respiration, 18. He was restless and wakeful during the early part of the night, but after 12 (midnight) slept well until morning. His general condition appears more encouraging.

D. W. BLISS,
FRANK H. HAMILTON.

ELBERON, N. J.,
September 8, 1881.

6 P. M.

At 12 M. to-day the President's temperature was 98.4°; pulse, 94; respiration, 17. At the evening dressing, 5.30 P. M., his temperature was 99.1°; pulse, 100; respiration, 18. He has taken a liberal amount of food (both solid and fluid) with apparent relish.

By special request of the President it has been made our duty to say, in this public manner, to Surgeon-General J. K. Barnes, Surgeon J. J. Woodward, and Dr. Robert Reyburn, that, in dispensing temporarily with their services as his medical attendants, he was actuated only by a wish to relieve them of a labor and responsibility which in his improved condition he could no longer properly impose upon them. Both the President and Mrs. Garfield desire us to express to these gentlemen personally, and in this same public manner, their high appreciation of the great skill and discretion which they have so constantly exercised as associate counsel in the management of his case up to the present time.

D. W. BLISS,
FRANK H. HAMILTON.

Elberon, N. J.,
September 9, 1881.

8.30 a. m.

At the examination of the President at 8 a. m., the temperature was 98.5°; pulse, 100; respiration, 17. The conditions of the parotid and wound are improving; he was somewhat wakeful during the night, but not restless, and slept sufficiently. The enemata and stimulants have been suspended during the past thirty-six hours. On the whole, the past twenty-four hours give evidence of favorable progress.

D. W. BLISS,
FRANK H. HAMILTON.

Elberon, N. J.,
September 9, 1881.

6 p. m.

At the examination of the President at 12 m. to-day, the temperature was 98.4°; pulse, 100; respiration, 17. At the evening dressing, at 5.30 p. m., the temperature was 98.8°; pulse, 100; respiration, 18.

It is believed, without referring to the records, that this is the first day since the development of the traumatic fever that the temperature, pulse, and respiration have been so nearly normal and uniform throughout the entire day.

D. W. BLISS,
FRANK H. HAMILTON,
D. HAYES AGNEW.

ELBERON, N. J.,
September 10, 1881.
9 A. M.

At the examination of the President at 8.30 this A. M., the temperature was 99.4°; pulse, 104; respiration, 18. He slept well during the night, awakening only at intervals of one-half to one hour. There is a perceptible increase of strength with an improved condition of the digestive apparatus. The tumefaction of the parotid has entirely disappeared, and the suppuration greatly diminished. The wound continues to improve, and presents a more healthy appearance.

D. W. BLISS.
D. HAYES AGNEW.

ELBERON, N. J.,
September 10, 1881.
6 P. M.

At the examination of the President at 12 M to-day his temperature was 98.5°; pulse, 100; respiration, 18. At 5.30 this evening his temperature was 98.7°; pulse, 100; respiration, 18. The President has taken a greater amount of liquid, with some solid food, and with more relish than for several days. His general condition is quite as favorable as yesterday.

D. W. BLISS,
D. HAYES AGNEW

ELBERON, N. J.,
September 11, 1881.
9 A. M.

At the examination of the President at 8.30 this A. M. his temperature was 98.8°; pulse, 104; respiration, 19. He was more restless, and the febrile rise later than on the preceding night. He continues to take sufficient nourishment without gastric disturbance.

D. W. BLISS,
D. HAYES AGNEW.

Elberon, N. J.,
September 11, 1881.

6 p. m.

The President has passed a quiet day, although the temperature has been somewhat higher and his pulse more frequent than during the previous twenty-four hours. At the evening dressing quite a large slough of connective tissue was removed from the region of the parotid,
He continues to take a sufficient quantity of nourishment, and enjoys it. At the noon examination his temperature was 100°; pulse, 110 ; respiration, 20. At the evening dressing his temperature was 100.6°; pulse, 110 ; respiration, 20.

D. W. BLISS,
D. HAYES AGNEW.

Elberon, N. J.,
September 12, 1881.

9 a. m.

The President passed an unusually good night, his sleep being uninterrupted, except occasionally to enable him to take nourishment. The suppuration from the parotid has almost entirely ceased ; the openings from which the pus discharged are rapidly healing.
The cough is less and the expectoration materially diminished. Temperature, 98.4°; pulse, 100 ; respiration, 18.

D. W. BLISS,
D. HAYES AGNEW.

Elberon, N. J.,
September 12, 1881.

6 p. m.

The President has experienced since the issue of the morning bulletin further amelioration of symptoms. He has been able to take an ample amount of food without discomfort, and has had several refreshing naps. At the noon examination the temperature was 99,2°; pulse 106; respiration, 20. At 5.30 p. m. the temperature was 98,6°; pulse, 100; respiration, 18.

D. W. BLISS,
D. HAYES AGNEW.

Elberon, N. J.,
September 13, 1881.

8.30 a. m.

At the examination of the President at 8 a. m. to-day the temperature was 99.4°; pulse, 100; respiration, 20. He passed a comfortable night, sleeping most of the time, and, on the whole, his condition this morning is more encouraging and gives promise of a good day.

D. W. BLISS,
FRANK H. HAMILTON.

Elberon, N. J.,
September 13, 1881.

6 p. m.

At the examination of the President at 12 m. to-day the temperature was 98.8°; pulse, 100; respiration, 20. At the evening dressing, 5.30 p. m., the temperature was 98.4° pulse, 100; respiration, 20. The President was placed in a semi-recumbent position upon an invalid-chair at 11 a. m., and remained one-half hour without fatigue or discomfort. The wounds are making the usual favorable progress, and his general condition is reassuring.

D. W. BLISS,
FRANK H. HAMILTON.

ELBERON. N. J.,
September 14, 1881.

9 A. M.

At the examination of the President at 8.30 this morning the temperature was 98.4°; pulse, 100; respiration, 19. He passed the night comfortably, sleeping sufficiently. He is bright and cheerful this morning, and has taken fruits and his first meal for the day with relish.

D. W. BLISS,
FRANK H. HAMILTON.

ELBERON, N. J.,
September 14, 1881.

6.30 P. M.

At the examination of the President at 12 M. to day his temperature was 98.8°; pulse, 104; respiration, 20. At the evening dressing, 5.30 P. M., the temperature was 99.2°; pulse, 112; respiration, 21. The President was placed on the invalid-chair, in a semi-reclining position, about 12 M., and remained one hour and a half, sleeping a part of the time. He was not fatigued by the transfer or change of position, and his general condition this evening is as favorable as usual notwithstanding a slight febrile rise.

D. W. BLISS,
FRANK H. HAMILTON,
D. HAYES AGNEW.

ELBERON, N. J.,
September 15, 1881.

9 A. M.

At the morning dressing, 8.30 to-day, the President's temperature was 98.4°; pulse, 100; respiration, 20. He passed the night comfortably, sleeping until 3 A. M., when he was wakeful for a period of two hours, during which time the pulse rose to 120, but without the marked elevation of temperature which has characterized the febrile disturbance heretofore. After this time he slept quietly until morning. More nourishment was given during the night than for several nights past. In reviewing the case of the President since his arrival at Long Branch it may be said that in spite of the various sceptic accidents which have for several weeks, and do still, complicate his case, he has certainly not retrograded, but, on the contrary, has made some progress towards convalescence.

D. W. BLISS,
FRANK H. HAMILTON,
D. HAYES AGNEW.

ELBERON, N. J.,
September, 15, 1881.

6 P. M.

The President has passed a quiet day, sleeping a little; has coughed occasionally, the expectoration being less purulent. A greater quantity of nourishment has been taken without discomfort. He was placed upon the invalid-chair and remained forty-five minutes in a position a little more elevated than on previous occasions. At 12 M. to-day his temperature was 98.9°; pulse, 102; respiration, 21. At the evening dressing, 5.30 P. M., the temperature was 99.2°; pulse, 104; respiration, 21.

D. W. BLISS,
FRANK H. HAMILTON,
D. HAYES AGNEW.

ELBERON, N. J.,
September 16, 1881.

9 A. M.

At the examination of the President at 8.30 this morning the temperature was 98.6°; pulse, 104; respiration, 21.

The febrile rise during the night was not so pronounced as it usually has been. There was, at times, considerable acceleration of pulse. He, however, slept comparatively well and took stimulants and nourishment as directed. The cough was somewhat more troublesome during the first part of the night, and the expectoration rather more purulent. The discharge from the wound is less abundant and not quite so healthy in appearance. The pulse, however, has more volume, and his general condition does not seem to have materially changed in any respect.

D. W. BLISS,
FRANK H. HAMILTON.

ELBERON, N. J.,
September 16, 1881.

6 P. M.

At the examination of the President at 12 M. to-day the temperature was 99.8°; pulse, 116; respiration, 21. At the evening dressing, at 5.30 P. M., the temperature was 98.6°; pulse, 104; respiration, 22. A slight febrile rise occurred at 11 A. M., and had entirely subsided at 2 o'clock P. M. The condition of the wound remains unchanged; the cough has not been so frequent or persistent, but the sputa still remains purulent. Nourishment and stimulants have been given in increased quantities without discomfort. Altogether his general condition cannot be said to be improved.

D. W. BLISS,
FRANK H. HAMILTON,
D. HAYES AGNEW.

ELBERON, N. J.,
September 17, 1881.

9 A. M.

At the morning examination and dressing of the President the temperature was 99.8°; pulse, 108, and respiration, 21.

The fluctuations of the pulse during the night varied from 116 to 130, the temperature during this time not deviating much from normal.

He slept quite well, taking nourishment at proper intervals. His cough was not troublesome, and the expectoration moderate. The discharge from the wound is more healthy, and the color of the granulations slightly improved.

D. W. BLISS,
D. HAYES AGNEW.

ELBERON, N. J.,
September 17, 1881.

6 P. M.

At the examination of the President at 12 M. to-day the temperature was 100.2°; pulse, 120; respiration, 24.

At 11.30 he had a severe chill, lasting half an hour, followed by perspiration. Since the noon examination there has been a gradual fall of temperature, with diminished frequency of pulse and respiration, so that at the evening examination the temperature was 98°: pulse, 102; respiration, 18.

He has slept most of the time during the afternoon and has taken his nourishment at proper intervals. The cough has been less frequent than usual.

D. W. BLISS,
D. HAYES AGNEW.

LONG BRANCH, N. J.,
September 18, 1881.

9 A. M.

At the examination of the President at 8.30 this A. M. the temperature was 98°; pulse, 102; respiration, 18. There was no perceptible febrile rise during the night, the pulse ranging from 102 to 112.

The cough was less troublesome than on previous nights, and the expectoration unchanged. He is able to take the nourishment and stimulants required without gastric disturbance nor has there been evidence of mental aberration during the night.

D. W. BLISS,
FRANK H. HAMILTON,
D. HAYES AGNEW.

ELBERON, N. J.,
September 18, 1881.

6 P. M.

The President, though quite weak, has passed a very quiet day. There has been no recurrence of chill nor mental disturbance. At 9 A. M. a slight febrile rise took place and began to subside at 11 o'clock, at which time the temperature was 100°; pulse, 116; respiration, 20. There has been no increase of cough or change in character of the expectoration. At the evening examination, at 5.30 P. M., the temperature was 98.4°; pulse, 102; respiration, 20.

D. W. BLISS,
D. HAYES AGNEW.

ELBERON, N. J.,
September 19, 1881.

9 A. M.

The condition of the President this morning continues unfavorable. Shortly after the issue of the evening bulletin he had a chill, lasting fifteen minutes. The febrile rise following continued until 12 midnight, during which time the pulse ranged from 112 to 130. The sweating that followed was quite profuse. The cough, which was troublesome during the chill, gave him but little annoyance the remainder of the night. This morning, at 8 A. M., the temperature was 98.8°; pulse, 106 and feeble; respiration, 22. At 8.30 another chill came on, on account of which the dressing was temporarily postponed. A bulletin will be issued at 12.30 P. M.

D. W. BLISS,
D. HAYES AGNEW.

ELBERON, N. J.,
September 19, 1881.

12.30 P. M.

The chill from which the President was suffering at the time the morning bulletin was issued lasted about fifteen minutes, and was followed by febrile rise of temperature and sweating.

He has slept much of the time, but his general condition has not materially changed since. Temperature, 98.2°; pulse, 104 ; respiration, 20.

D. W. BLISS,
D. HAYES AGNEW.

ELBERON, N. J.,
September 19, 1881.

6 P. M.

Though the gravity of the President's condition continues, there has been no aggravation of symptoms since the noon bulletin was issued. He has slept most of the time, coughing but little, and with more ease. The sputa remains unchanged. A sufficient amount of nourishment has been taken and retained.

Temperature, 98.4°; pulse, 102 ; respiration, 18.

D. W. BLISS,
FRANK H. HAMILTON,
D. HAYES AGNEW.

ELBERON, N. J.,
September 19, 1881.

11.30 P. M.

The President died at 10.35 P. M. After the bulletin was issued, at 5.30 this evening, the President continued in much the same condition as during the afternoon, the pulse varying from 100 to 106, with rather increased force and volume.

After taking nourishment he fell into a quiet sleep. About thirty-five minutes before his death, and while asleep, his pulse rose to 120, and was somewhat more feeble. At 10 o'clock he awoke, complaining of a severe pain above the region of his heart. He almost immediately became unconscious, and ceased to breathe at 10.35.

D. W. BLISS,
FRANK H. HAMILTON,
D. HAYES AGNEW.

FULL OFFICIAL REPORT OF THE AUTOPSY.

Official record of the post-mortem examination of the body of President James A. Garfield, made September 20, 1881, commencing at 4.30 P. M., eighteen hours after death, at Francklyn Cottage, Elberon, N. J. Present and assisting Dr. D. W. Bliss, Surgeon-General J. K. Barnes, Surgeon J. J. Woodward, U. S. A., Dr. Robert Reyburn, Dr. Frank H. Hamilton, Dr. D. Hayes Agnew, Dr. Andrew H. Smith, of Elberon, (and New York), and Acting Assistant Surgeon D. S. Lamb, of the Army Medical Museum, Washington, D. C.

Before commencing the examination a consultation was held by these physicians in a room adjoining that in which the body lay, and it was unanimously agreed that the dissection should be made by Dr. Lamb, and that Surgeon Woodward should record the observations made. It was further unanimously agreed that the cranium should not be opened. Surgeon Woodward then proposed that the examination should be conducted as follows:

That the body should be viewed externally, and any morbid appearances existing recorded. That a catheter should then be passed into the wound, as was done during life, to wash it out for the purpose of assisting to find the position of the bullet. That a long incision should next be made from the superior extremity of the sternum to the pubis, and this crossed by a transverse one just below the umbilicus. That the abdominal flaps thus made should then be turned back and the abdominal viscera examined. That after the abdominal cavity was opened the position of the bullet should be ascertained if possible before making any further incision, and that finally the thoracic viscera should be examined. This order of procedure was unanimously agreed to.

The examination was then proceeded with, and the following external appearances were observed: The body was considerably emaciated, but the face was much less wasted than the limbs. A preservative fluid had been injected by the embalmer a few hours before into the left femoral artery. The pipes used for the purpose were still in position. The anterior surface of the body presented no abnormal appearances, and there was no ecchymosis or other discoloration of any part of the front of the abdomen. Just below the right ear, and a little behind it, there was an oval ulcerated opening about half an inch in diameter, from which some sanious pus was escaping, but no tumefaction could be observed in the parotid region.

A considerable number of purpura-like spots were scattered thickly over the left scapula, and thence forward as far as the axilla. They ranged from one-eighth to one-fourth of an inch in diameter, were slightly elevated, and furfuraceous on the surface, and many of them were confluent in groups of two to four or more. A similar but much less abundant eruption was observed sparsely scattered over the corresponding region on the right side. An oval excavated ulcer about an inch long, the result of a small carbuncle, was seated over the spinous process of the tenth dorsal vertebra. Over the sacrum there were four small bed sores, the largest about half an inch in diameter. A few acne pustules and a number of irregular spots of post-mortem hypostatic congestion were scattered over the shoulders, back, and buttocks. The inferior part of the scrotum was much discolored by hypostatic congestion. A group of hemorrhoidal tumors, rather larger than a walnut, protruded from the anus.

The depressed cicatrix of the wound made by the pistol-bullet was recognized over the tenth intercostal space, three and a half inches to the right of the vertebral spines. A deep linear incision (made in part by the operation of July 24 and extended by that of August 8) occupied a position closely corresponding to the upper border of the right twelfth rib. It commenced posteriorly, about two inches from the vertebral spines and extended forward a little more than three inches. At the anterior extremity of this incision there was a deep, nearly square, abraded surface about an inch across.

A well-oiled, flexible catheter, fourteen inches long, was then passed into this wound, as had been done to wash it out during life. More resistance was at first encountered than had usually been the case, but after several trials the catheter entered without any violence to its full length. It was then left in position and the body disposed supinely for the examination of the viscera.

The cranium was not opened.

A long incision was made from the superior extremity of the sternum to the pubis, followed by a transverse incision crossing the abdomen just below the umbilicus. The four flaps thus formed were turned back and the abdominal viscera exposed. The subcutaneous adipose tissue, divided by the incisions, was little more than one-eighth of an inch thick over the thorax, but was thicker over the abdomen, being about a quarter of an inch along the linea alba, and as much as half an inch thick towards the outer extremity of the transverse incision. On inspection of the abdominal viscera *in situ* the transverse colon was observed to lie a little above the line of the umbilicus. It was firmly adherent to the anterior edge of the liver. The greater omentum covered the intestines pretty thoroughly from the transverse colon almost to the pubis. It was still quite fat and was very much blackened by venous congestion. On both sides its lateral margins were adherent to the abdominal parietes opposite the eleventh and twelfth ribs. On the left side the adhesions were numerous, firm, well-organized, and probably old. (A foot-note here says: These adhesions and the firm ones on the right side, as well as those of the spleen, possibly date back to an attack of chronic dysentery, from which the patient is said to have suffered during the civil war.) On the right side there were a few similar adhesions and a number of more delicate and probably recent ones.

A mass of black coagulated blood covered and concealed the spleen and the left margin of the greater omentum. On raising the omentum it was found that this blood mass extended through the left lumbar and iliac regions and dipped down into the pelvis, in which there was some clotted blood and rather more than a pint of bloody fluid. (A foot note here says: A large part of this fluid had probably transuded from the injecting material of the embalmer.) The blood coagula, having been turned out and collected, measured very nearly a pint. It was now evident that secondary hemorrhage had been the immediate cause of death, but the point from which the blood had escaped was not at once apparent. The omentum was not adherent to the intestines, which were moderately distended with gas. No intestinal adhesions were found other than those between the transverse colon and the liver already mentioned.

The abdominal cavity being now washed out as thoroughly as possible, a fruitless attempt was made to obtain some indication of the position of the bullet before making any further incision. By pushing the intestines aside the extremity of the catheter which had been passed into the wound could be felt between the peritoneum and the right iliac fascia, but it had evidently doubled upon itself, and although a prolonged search was made, nothing could be seen or felt to indicate the presence of the bullet, either in that region or elsewhere. The abdominal viscera were then carefully removed from the body, placed in suitable vessels, and examined *seriatim*, with the following result: The adhesions between the liver and transverse colon proved to bound an abscess cavity between the under surface of the liver, the transverse colon and the transverse meso-colon, which involved the gall bladder and extended to about the same distance on each side of it, measuring six inches transversely, and four inches from before backward. This cavity was lined by a thick pyogenic membrane which completely replaced the capsule of that part of the under surface of the liver occupied by the abscess. It contained about two ounces of greenish-yellow fluid, a mixture of pus and biliary matter. This abscess did not involve any portion of the substance of the liver except the surface with which it was in contact, and no cummunication could be detected between it and any part of the wound.

Some recent peritoneal adhesions existed between the upper surface of the right lobe of the liver and the diaphragm. The liver was larger than normal, weighing eighty-four ounces. Its substance was firm, but of a pale yellowish color on its surface and throughout the interior of the organ from fatty degeneration. No evidence that it had been penetrated by the bullet could be found, nor were there any abscesses or infarctions in any part of its tissue. The spleen was connected to the diaphragm by firm, probably old, peritoneal adhesions. There were several rather deep congenital fissures in its margins, giving it a lobulated appearance. It was abnormally large, weighing eighteen ounces, of a very dark, lake-red color, both on the surface and on section. Its parenchyma was soft and flabby, but contained no abcesses or infarctions. There were some recent peritoneal adhesions between the posterial wall of the stomach and the posterior abdominal parietes. With this exception no abnormities were discovered in the stomach or intestines, nor were any other evidences of general or local peritonitis found besides those already specified.

The right kidney weighed six ounces, the left kidney seven. Just beneath the capsule of the left kidney, at about the middle of its convex border, there was a little abscess one-third of an inch in diameter. There were three small serious cysts on the convex border of the right kidney just beneath its capsule. In other respects the tissue of both kidneys was normal in appearance and in texture.

The urinary bladder was empty. Behind the right kidney, after the removal of that organ from the body, the dilated track of the bullet was dissected into. It was found that from the point at which it had fractured the right eleventh rib (three inches and a half to the right of the vertebral spines) the missile had gone to the left, obliquely forward, passing through the body of the first lumbar vertebra, and lodging in the adipose connective tissue immediately below the lower border of the pancreas, about two inches and a half to the left of the spinal column and behind the peritoneum. It had become completely encysted.

The track of the bullet, between the point at which it had fractured the eleventh rib and that at which it entered the first lumbar vertebra, was considerably dilated, and the pus had burrowed downward through the adipose tissue behind the right kidney, and thence had found its way between the peritoneum and the right iliac fascia, making a descending channel, which extended almost to the groin. The adipose tissue behind the kidney, in the vicinity of the descending channel, was much thickened and condensed by inflammation. In the channel, which was found almost free from pus, lay the flexible catheter introduced into the wound at the commencement of the autopsy; its extremity was found doubled upon itself immediately beneath the pertioneum, reposing upon the iliac fascia, where the channel was dilated into a pouch of considerable size. This long descending channel, now clearly seen to have been caused by the burrowing of pus from the wound, was supposed during life to have been the track of the bullet.

The last dorsal, together with the first and second lumbar vertebræ and the twelfth rib, were then removed from the body for more thorough examination.

When the examination was made it was found that the bullet had penetrated the first lumbar vertebra in the upper part of the right side of its body. The aperture by which it entered involved the intervertebral cartilage next above, and was situated just below and anterior to the intervertebra foramen, from which its upper margin was about one-quarter of an inch distant. Passing obliquely to the left and forward through the upper part of the body of the first lumbar vertebra, the bullet emerged by an aperture, the center of which was about half an inch to the left of the median line,

and which also involved the intervertebral cartilage next
above. The cancellated tissue of the body of the first lumbar
vertebra was very much comminuted, and the fragments
somewhat displaced. Several deep fissures extended from
the track of the bullet to the lower part of the body of the
twelfth dorsal vertebra, others extended through the first
lumbar vertebra into the intervertebral cartilage between it
and the second lumbar vertebra. Both this cartilage and
that next above were partly destroyed by ulceration. A
number of minute fragments from the fractured lumbar
vertebra had been driven into the adjacent soft parts.

It was further found that the right twelfth rib also was
fractured at a point one inch and a quarter to the right of
the transverse process of the twelfth dorsal vetrebra. This
injury had not been recognized during life.

On sawing through the vertebra, a little to the right of
the median line, it was found that the spinal canal was not
involved by the track of the ball. The spinal cord and
other contents of this portion of the spinal canal presented
no abnormal appearances. The rest of the spinal cord was
not examined.

Beyond the first lumbar vertebra the bullet continued to
go to the left, passing behind the pancreas to the point
where it was found. Here it was enveloped in a firm cyst of
connective tissue, which contained, besides the ball, a minute
quantity of inspissated somewhat cheesy pus, which formed
a thin layer over a portion of the surface of the lead. There
was also a black shred adherent to a part of the cyst wall,
which proved, on microscopical examination, to be the
remains of a blood clot. For about an inch from this cyst,
the track of the ball behind the pancreas was completely
obliterated by the healing process, thence as far backward
as the body of the first lumbar vertebra the track was filled
with coagulated blood, which extended on the left into an irregular space rent in the adjoining adipose tissue behind the peritoneum and above the pancreas. The blood had worked its
way to the left, bursting finally through the peritoneum

behind the spleen into the abdominal cavity. The rending of the tissue by the extravasation of this blood was undoubtedly the cause of the paroxysms of pain which occurred a short time before death. This mass of coagulated blood was of irregular form, and nearly as large as a man's fist. It could be distinctly seen from in front, through the peritoneum, after its site behind the greater curvature of the stomach had been exposed by the dissection of the greater omentum from the stomach, and especially after some delicate adhesions between the stomach and the part of the peritoneum covering the blood mass had been broken down by the fingers. From the relations of the mass as thus seen it was believed that the hemorrhage had proceeded from one of the mesenteric arteries, but as it was clear that a minute dissection would be required to determine the particular branch involved, it was agreed that the infiltrated tissues and the adjoining soft parts should be preserved for subsequent study.

On the examination and dissection, made in accordance with this agreement, it was found that the fatal hemorrhage proceeded from a rent nearly four-tenths of an inch long in the main trunk of the splenic artery, two inches and a half to the left of the coeliac axis. This rent must have occurred at least several days before death, since the everted edges in the slit in the vessel were united by firm adhesions to the surrounding connective tissue, thus forming an almost continuous wall bounding the adjoining portion of the blood-clot. Moreover, the peripheral portion of the clot in this vicinity was disposed in pretty firm concentric layers. It was further found that the cyst below the lower margin of the pancreas, in which the bullet was found, was situated three inches and a half to the left of the coeliac axis. Besides the mass of coagulated blood just described, another about the size of a walnut was found in the greater omentum, near the splenic extremity of the stomach. The communication, if any, between this and the larger hemorrhagic mass could not be made out.

The examination of the thoracic viscera resulted as follows: The heart weighed eleven ounces. All the cavities were entirely empty except the right ventricle, in which a few shreds of soft, reddish coagulated blood adhered to the internal surface. On the surface of the mitral valve there were several spots of fatty degeneration; with this exception the cardiac valves were normal. The muscular tissue of the heart was soft and tore easily. A few spots of fatty degeneration existed in the lining membrane of the aorta, just above the semilunar valves, and a slender clot of fibrin was found in the aorta, where it was divided about two inches from these valves for the removal of the heart.

On the right side slight pleuritic adhesions existed between the convex surface of the lower lobe of the lung and the costal pleura, and firm adhesions between the anterior edge of the lower lobe, the pericardium, and the diaphragm. The right lung weighed thirty-two ounces. The posterior part of the fissure, between its upper and lower lobes, was congenitally incomplete. The lower lobe of the right lung was hypostatically congested, and considerable portions, especially toward its base, were the seat of broncho pneumonia. The bronchial tubes contained a considerable quantity of stringy muco pus, their mucous surface was reddened by catarrhal bronchitis. The lung tissue was œdematous; (a foot-note here says: a part at least of this condition was doubtless due to the extravasation of the injecting fluid used by the embalmer,) but contained no abcesses or infarctions.

On the left side the lower lobe of the lung was bound behind to the costal pleura, above to the upper lobe, and below to the diaphragm by pretty firm pleuritic adhesions. The left lung weighed twenty-seven ounces. The condition of its bronchial tubes and of the lung tissue was very nearly the same as on the right side, the chief difference being that the area of broncho pneumonia in the lower lobe was much less extensive in the left lung than in the right. In the lateral part of the lower lobe of the left lung, and about an inch from its plural surface there was a group of four minute areas of gray hepatization, each about one eighth of an inch in diamater. There were no infarctions and no abscesses in any part of the lung tissue.

The surgeons assisting at the autopsy were unanimously of the opinion that on reviewing the history of the case in connection with the autopsy, it is quite evident that the different suppurating surfaces and especially the fractured spongy tissue of the vertebra, furnish a sufficient explanation of the sceptic conditions which existed during life. About an hour after the post-mortem examination was completed the physicians named at the commencement of this report assembled for further consultation in an adjoining cottage. A brief outline of the results of the post-mortem examination was drawn up, signed by all the physicians, and handed to Private Secretary J. Stanley Brown, who was requested to furnish copies to the newspaper press.

D. W. BLISS,
J. K. BARNES,
J. J. WOODWARD,
ROBT. REYBURN,
D. S. LAMB.

As the above report contains paragraphs detailing the observations made at Washington on the pathological specimens preserved for that purpose, the names of Drs. F. H. Hamilton, D. Hayes Agnew, and A. H. Smith are not appended to it. It has, however, been submitted to them, and they have given their assent to the other portions of the report.

OFFICIAL BULLETIN OF THE AUTOPSY.

Long Branch, N. J.,
September 20, 1881.

By previous arrangement a post-mortem examination of the body of President Garfield was made this afternoon, in the presence and with the assistance of Drs. Hamilton, Agnew, Bliss, Barnes, Woodward, Reyburn, Andrew H. Smith, of Elberon, and Acting Assistant Surgeon D. S. Lamb, of the Army Medical Museum, of Washington. The operation was performed by Dr. Lamb. It was found that the ball, after fracturing the right eleventh rib, had passed through the spinal column in front of the spinal cord, fracturing the body of the first lumbar vertebra, driving a number of small fragments of bone into the adjacent soft parts, and lodging below the pancreas, about two inches and a half to the left of the spine, and behind the peritoneum, where it had become completely encysted.

The immediate cause of death was secondary hemorrhage from one of the mesenteric arteries adjoining the track of the ball, the blood rupturing the peritoneum, and nearly a pint escaping into the abdominal cavity. This hemorrhage is believed to have been the cause of the severe pain in the lower part of the chest complained of just before death. An abscess-cavity, six inches by four in dimensions, was found in the vicinity of the gall-bladder, between the liver and the transverse colon, which were strongly adherent. It did not involve the substance of the liver, and no communication was found between it and the wound.

A long, suppurating channel extended from the external wound, between the loin muscles and the right kidney, almost to the right groin. This channel, now known to be due to the burrowing of pus from the wound, was supposed, during life, to have been the track of the ball.

On an examination of the organs of the chest evidences of severe bronchitis were found on both sides, with bronchopneumonia of the lower portions of the right lung, and, though to a much less extent, of the left. The lungs contained no abscesses, and the heart no clots. The liver was enlarged and fatty, but not from abscesses. Nor were any found in any other organ, except the left kidney, which contained, near its surface, a small abscess about one-third of an inch in diameter.

In reviewing the history of the case in connection with the autopsy, it is quite evident that the different suppurating surfaces, and especially the fractured spongy tissue of the vertebrae, furnish a sufficient explanation of the septic condition which existed.

D. W. BLISS,   FRANK H. HAMILTON.
J. K. BARNES,   D. HAYES AGNEW.
J. J. WOODWARD,   ANDREW H. SMITH.
ROBERT REYBURN.   D. S. LAMB.

www.ingramcontent.com/pod-product-compliance
Lightning Source LLC
Chambersburg PA
CBHW031404160426
43196CB00007B/892